AF263980

PRAISE FOR *EMPOWER YOUR MARKETING*

"Sacha Awwa has written more than a mere marketing manual; she has crafted a mirror for the modern entrepreneur. Most confusion about marketing comes from a business identity crisis or a lack of clarity about who the business is and why it exists. Awwa's framework acts as a grounding technique, stripping away the fear and anxiety of 'What should I do?' and replacing it with the clarity of 'Who am I serving?' with practical exercises every step of the way. By integrating marketing into the very soul of the business mission, she helps leaders move from a state of reactive indecision or dispassionate throwing of money at the problem to a state of purposeful, authentic connection. This is essential reading for any business owner looking to quiet the chaos and find their center through the lens of marketing."

— **Dr. Adam Formal**, Clinical Psychologist and Founder of Formal Therapy, Director of Mental Health for Team USA, Maccabi USA

"I've had a front-row seat to Sacha using the 3P framework to transform businesses. Prepare, Propel, Perfect isn't just a concept—it's a system that works. Too many companies overlook the building blocks and end up spending tens of thousands fixing preventable mistakes. This book helps business owners get it right the first time."

— **Michael A. DiLillo**, former Senior Marketing Manager at fuboTV

"Right from the start, *Empower Your Marketing* clarifies its purpose. Instead of piling on more chatter, it aims to cut through it, which immediately stands out. The author quickly addresses the busy entrepreneurs who are lost in a sea of strategies, tools, and claims that rarely work. What caught my eye first is how clearly things are communicated: Marketing isn't confusing—it's drowned out. With everything now filtered through AI, social noise, and endless updates, creating space for genuine signals becomes essential.

The 3P method isn't just a plan; it brings order and provides clear direction, building confidence. When leaders know their craft well but struggle with promotion, this clarity can elevate their position. Notably, the book is based on real conversations with actual entrepreneurs, not just abstract ideas; it's been proven in practice. The emphasis on truth, flexibility, and shared connection shifts the perspective: Marketing is about people, not tactics.

If you're a founder feeling overwhelmed by a flood of choices and unsure which path to take, this book doesn't trumpet tricks; instead, it offers quiet support. That steady foundation is where lasting progress begins. This feels less like a book that simply teaches and more like one that keeps you grounded."

— **Andre Flax**, former Regional VP of Sales at Yelp

EMPOWER YOUR MARKETING

Master the Basics, Stop Wasting Money,

Fast Track Your Growth

EMPOWER

YOUR

MARKETING

SACHA AWWA

Podcast Host of **Uncomplicated** Marketing

This book is dedicated to:

Carin Awwa

Arfan Awwa

Samer Awwa

Archie (Woof!)

To my family (and puppy) who stood beside me and believed in me as I dedicated countless days and hours to completing this book: your encouragement sustained me through the challenges and celebrated with me during the breakthroughs. Your unwavering support has been my foundation throughout this journey

Nancy Marriott

Your wisdom transformed my vision and words into something greater than I could have possibly imagined. This book bears the invisible imprint of our collaboration, and for that partnership, I am eternally grateful.

My friends

To my friends who have stood by me through every challenge and celebration (you know who you are), thank you for seeing potential in me and for the countless ways your unwavering belief has helped transform possibility into reality.

CONTENTS

BREAKING THROUGH THE MARKETING NOISE

After two decades of helping entrepreneurs and businesses just like yours navigate the marketing maze, I'm about to share something that might shock you: Marketing isn't as complex as you've been led to believe. It's simply a noisy platform, which creates overwhelming confusion for consumers and entrepreneurs.

Education is the key to all things, and this book provides clarity for anyone involved in the marketing process, regardless of their level of expertise. It's for marketing experts seeking a more streamlined direction in approaching and supporting their clients. It's for in-house marketers and executives who want to better understand what their marketing teams are doing. And, most importantly, it's for entrepreneurs who find marketing overwhelming and confusing and want clarity to help their business run better. After all, entrepreneurs and business owners like you are part of an elite powerhouse that makes up 90 percent of all businesses worldwide[1] and provides 50 percent[2] of global employment. You deserve a practical approach to marketing that actually works for real businesses, like yours.

Why Marketing Is so Challenging Today

Picture this: You're a business owner who's mastered your craft. You are the backbone of your community, creating jobs, driving innovation, and fueling opportunity. You've created something remarkable—a product or service that genuinely fills a market gap. But with this job comes unique challenges—limited resources, tight budgets, and the relentless pressure to achieve more with less. And when it comes to marketing, you feel trapped in a maze of conflicting advice, endless options, and expensive solutions that don't quite deliver.

The marketing world is saturated with voices vying for your attention, creating confusion rather than clarity. You want to make the best choice that will help your business, but you don't know what it needs. Social media, email campaigns, or search engine optimization (SEO)—you've been told these are all important, but without knowing the complete picture, a marketing

---

1   World Bank, "Small and Medium Enterprises (SMEs) Finance," *World Bank*, accessed October 21, 2025, https://www.worldbank.org/en/topic/smefinance.

2   Julia Devos and Zishu Chen, "Why We Shouldn't Overlook the Impact of SMEs on Local and Global Economies," *World Economic Forum*, August 29, 2022, accessed October 21, 2025, https://www.weforum.org/stories/2022/08/why-we-shouldn-t-overlook-the-impact-of-smes-on-local-and-global-economies-105d723ec7/.

expert that's hyper-focused on perfecting one individual piece of the marketing puzzle won't take you very far.

Sometimes, your choice for marketing power is made for you—whichever company has the most market share and is making the loudest noise gets your business. In today's world, especially as our businesses are amplified by the rapid rise of AI and ever-evolving technologies, this noise is only getting louder.

My Mission: The 3P Framework

My mission is to cut through all that noise and provide you with the clarity you need to build sustainable, long-term success. I've developed a simple, practical way to approach marketing: the 3Ps, a cyclical framework that breaks down the complexities of marketing into clear, actionable steps:

1. **Prepare**: Putting down your foundation

2. **Propel**: Building out your strategy

3. **Perfect**: Executing and refining what's working and what's not

In a world where AI and technology are constantly shifting the business landscape, these foundational principles remain constant and powerful. Knowing them empowers you to make better choices. The goal isn't to turn you into a marketing expert. You already have enough on your plate mastering the craft of your business. Instead, I want to help you think like a marketer—more on the high level than in the weeds—while still acting like the entrepreneur you are.

Real-World Insights

What makes this book different is that it's built not just on theory, but real-world experience—both mine and what I've seen firsthand. As I cross into the second year of my *Uncomplicated Marketing* podcast, I've gathered fascinating insights from entrepreneurs across diverse industries—from leadership coaching to gaming, fintech to social impact. Many pivoted to entrepreneurship from unrelated backgrounds, allowing them to leverage their past experiences while learning entirely new skill sets. With this incredible diversity of industries, work experience, and personalities, I've discovered remarkable similarities across the founders' journeys: Nearly all successful entrepreneurs are driven by a strong *why* behind their business, and almost universally, they've found that authentic storytelling is their ultimate marketing tool.

Through dozens of interviews and hundreds of hours of discussions with founders, I've confirmed that though the core tactics in marketing remain similar, it isn't one-size-fits-all. The key differentiator for effective marketing is knowing your target audience and how you connect with their needs. What truly drives success is:

Authenticity: Connecting your personal experiences with your target audience's needs

Adaptability: Being willing to pivot based on real-world feedback from your consumers

Community: Building strong relationships with customers, partners, and mentors

Whether you're bootstrapping or seeking venture capital, launching quickly or developing methodically, the path to marketing success starts with clarity about your audience and your purpose.

How to Get the Most from This Book

To maximize your journey through this book and transform your marketing approach, I recommend keeping a notebook handy to jot down ideas and insights specific to your business. Inspiration strikes in the best ways as you learn, and a successful business is more likely to happen when you're prepared. To get started, here are three high-level items to keep in mind while reading:

1. **Start with Foundation First**. Think of marketing like building a house—you need a solid foundation before you do anything else. For marketers, that's starting with the crucial groundwork of understanding your audience. Each chapter builds upon the previous one, so don't skip ahead, even if you're tempted. This sequential approach will save you time and money in the long run. Even if your business is a couple of years old, you will need to understand the foundational aspects to optimize this book (and your business!)

2. **Learn the Three-Phase Framework**. The 3P framework isn't just theory—it's a practical approach that has helped businesses across every industry achieve sustainable growth. Like learning a new board game, marketing is fun when you know how to play. Understanding the rules and strategies is the first step toward playing effectively, and playing effectively means

winning. It also helps you recognize that marketing is a cycle—it never truly ends, but keeps evolving as you and your business grow.

3. **Embrace the Journey**. Marketing isn't a straight road with a clear destination. It's a dynamic and ongoing process. Remember, you don't need to become a marketing expert. You just need to understand enough to make informed decisions and work effectively with marketing professionals, who can support you along the way. Don't worry, I will guide you when and where you will need them in your journey. And so you know how to speak their language, I've provided a glossary of terms, acronyms, and assorted jargon for you to reference.

What to Expect

In the chapters that follow, we'll look at the foundations of your success and dive deeper into each phase of the 3P framework:

The Entrepreneurial Paradox (Chapter 1) – We'll explore what a year of conversations with entrepreneurs revealed about their journeys, examining the patterns that emerged across different industries and business models. You'll discover the common threads that cause entrepreneurs to stand in their own way of success and what strategies these businessmen and women took to put their companies on the right track to achieve their goals.

The Marketing Cycle: A New Approach (Chapter 2) – We'll focus on the high-level first, examining how to build a foundation that makes for a good and effective marketing plan. Without this, not even the best marketers can take a company to super stardom. After you're introduced to the 4Ws, the cyclical nature of marketing, and the customer journey, you'll be ready to go more in-depth into the 3Ps—your new marketing strategy.

Phase One: Prepare (Chapter 3) – We'll focus on understanding your audience at a personal level—their challenges, frustrations, and aspirations. You'll learn how to create a solid foundation for your marketing efforts by developing clear messaging that resonates with your target market.

Phase Two: Plan (Chapter 4) – We'll map out actionable strategies to reach your audience effectively. From selecting the right channels to crafting compelling content, you'll gain the tools to execute your marketing plan with confidence.

Phase Three: Perform (Chapter 5) – We'll explore how to measure what matters, refine your approach, and scale what works. You'll learn how to create a cycle of continuous improvement that drives sustainable growth.

This book is more than just another marketing guide—it's a mindset shift that you can use, whether you're launching your business or looking to refine your strategies, to break free from the cycle of confusion and noise.

You're not alone, and you're not behind. Let me empower you to transform your approach to marketing, one step at a time. Let's begin this journey together, and you'll discover how the right approach can not only reignite and establish your belief in marketing but also unlock the growth and success your business deserves.

CHAPTER 1

THE ENTREPRENEURIAL PARADOX

Know Thyself.

– Socrates

So let me start with a tough but necessary question: Are you standing in your own way?

I've worked alongside a kaleidoscope of entrepreneurs—visionaries, perfectionists, skeptics, and dreamers. But entrepreneurship is not without its unique challenges—limited resources, tight budgets, and the relentless pressure to achieve more with less. While the entrepreneurial spirit is undeniably magnetic, it can also be the very thing that throws a business off course. Sometimes, we—the founders—are our own biggest obstacle.

That's why I wrote this book. It's for business owners and leaders like you who are ready to break through the barriers holding you back—yourself included.

It's also for those who've felt the frustration of what you think of as failed marketing efforts and need a roadmap that's practical, clear, and proven. Entrepreneurs often find themselves steering off course when it comes to marketing. Why? Because they're relentlessly bombarded with pitches from companies eager to sell solutions, even when they might not be the right fit for their company's unique needs. This doesn't mean these aren't great tools or solutions—they may just not align with your business requirements.

The Balancing Act

Entrepreneurship is a balancing act. Some founders micromanage every detail, convinced that perfection lies in their grasp, while others delegate too freely, risking chaos and oversight. Striking the right balance between involvement and trust is critical. It's not about letting go completely or holding on too tightly. It's about knowing when to lead and when to let others take the reins.

Take, for example, a founder I worked with who had built a $15 million-a-year business over fifteen years. He became so consumed with crafting the perfect tweet that he couldn't focus on scaling his company further. On the flip side, I've seen founders whose lack of oversight led to significant breaches in security and morale. Somewhere in between hyperdetailed and too-far-removed is where success lives. Finding this balance requires grit.

When You're the Roadblock

The truth is this: Entrepreneurship isn't glamorous. It's messy. It's about showing up, doing the hard work, and "keeping consistent" even when the results feel far away. Success doesn't come overnight, but persistence—combined with smart strategy—will win in the end. This may be cliché, but the truth of consistency speaks volumes.

And success as an entrepreneur isn't just about what you do and how you do it; it's a lot about who you are and how you're showing up for your business and your team. Sometimes, the biggest shifts that bring about improvement come when we stop and check ourselves. So, how do you know when it's time to check yourself? Here is a set of cues to start with and how to address them:

Cue: Your team seems disengaged, or morale is low.

Fix: Reflect on whether your leadership style is fostering collaboration or creating unnecessary tension. Are you communicating your expectations clearly? Are you giving your team the support they need to succeed? If you are a one-man show, this goes without saying for yourself too. Remember, you may be treading the trenches alone, but one entrepreneur I had on my podcast said, "Ambition builds a founder, and asking for help builds a business." My personal mantra is "It takes a village." Asking for help and feedback is in no way a failure, so don't be afraid to do this when you feel like your progress is lagging.

Cue: You're overwhelmed with tasks others could handle.

Fix: Ask yourself if you're holding onto things out of fear of letting go. Or simply, are you really being too cheap to hire someone to take on the task? Delegating isn't a sign of weakness. It's a sign of trust. Sometimes you may not think you are ready to bring someone on, but at the end of the day, remember you are the brains behind the company—you need your time to be freed up to continue building. This is a mindset shift that will alter your perspective. When you actually let go, trust me—you will feel freer. It may be easier for some more than others, but find the tools to make this work! Also, be sure to check in with yourself. Your mental health is very important in this journey.

Cue: When making decisions, you feel paralyzed by overthinking.

Fix: Learn to prioritize progress over perfection. Perfection isn't always achievable or necessary. Remember, it's better to get to 80 percent than for it to take months or years to get to 100 percent. This is going to remain key throughout your business. You will miss out if you don't get it out, and trying to get it perfect will only keep you in the weeds for longer. This is a nasty cycle to be in, so break it now before it becomes hard to release.

Cue: Your business isn't growing as expected.
Fix: Reassess your strategies. Are you focusing on what truly moves the needle, or are you caught up in distractions?

If you're a solo entrepreneur, the process can feel even more daunting. Here are five simple steps to keep yourself on track and keep out of your own way:

1. **Set a weekly check-in with yourself.** Reflect on your progress, challenges, and wins. What's working? What's not?

2. **Prioritize your tasks daily.** Focus on three key things you need to accomplish. Don't overwhelm yourself with a never-ending to-do list.

3. **Find an accountability partner or mentor.** Even if you're working solo, having someone to bounce ideas off of or hold you accountable can make a huge difference. You can also join communities or coworking spaces to keep you going and build community.

4. **Celebrate small wins.** Don't wait for the big milestones to recognize your efforts. Acknowledge progress, no matter how small.

5. **Keep learning.** Dedicate time to building your knowledge, whether it's through books, courses, or podcasts. Growth requires continuous learning. Personally, podcasts kept me going when I started my business. They made me feel seen, and hearing others' experiences—especially their mistakes—helped me avoid pitfalls I could have easily fallen into.

What My Conversations Revealed

As I cross into the third year of my *Uncomplicated Marketing* podcast, I want to share what I've learned from dozens of interviews and hundreds of hours of discussions with founders across industries—from leadership coaching and gaming, to fintech and social impact. These conversations have revealed patterns that paint a fascinating picture of what drives entrepreneurial success in today's market—patterns you might recognize in your own journey.

Despite incredible diversity in industries and business models, I've been struck by the remarkable similarities in founders' journeys, challenges, and breakthroughs. These shared experiences cut across sector boundaries and revealed universal truths about the entrepreneurial path. Here are four common threads these businesses and entrepreneurs share:

1. **A Strong *Why* Behind the Business.** Almost universally, I've found that successful entrepreneurs aren't just chasing profit—they're chasing purpose. Many of my guests started their businesses because they felt deeply dissatisfied with their previous careers. They craved more meaningful work that aligned with their values and vision for their lives.

   What's particularly interesting is that many had a specific inciting moment—a catalyst that finally pushed them from idea to action. For some, it was burnout after years in a corporate environment. For others, it was suddenly seeing a market gap they couldn't unsee. These weren't gradual shifts. They were decisive moments of clarity that demanded action, giving them the *why* behind what they do.

2. **Pivoting from Unrelated Backgrounds.** I was struck by how many successful founders came from completely unrelated fields. One week, I'd be interviewing someone who left investment banking. The next, it was someone who abandoned a promising career in medicine or law. These entrepreneurs weren't traditional business founders—some pivoted to an entirely new industry, while others applied their professional expertise in new ways. But all of them brought their fresh perspectives as first-time company builders.

And what they all shared, despite their unrelated backgrounds, was the ability to leverage their past experience while simultaneously learning new skill sets. Many admitted that the hardest parts of business weren't the technical aspects, but rather the marketing and business development components. They knew their products or services inside and out, but reaching customers required an entirely different toolkit.

3. **The Power of Community and Networks.** If there's one lesson that came through in nearly every interview, it's that no entrepreneur succeeds alone. These entrepreneurs' business models were built around connection—whether that meant creating an engaged audience, fostering a passionate community, or cultivating relationships with investors and strategic partners.

   What surprised me was how often the most significant business breakthroughs came not from formal business strategies, but from organic connections. One founder mentioned how a casual conversation at a conference led to their biggest client. Another credited their rapid growth to word-of-mouth referrals from their very first customers who became enthusiastic advocates of their product.

4. **Storytelling as the Ultimate Marketing Tool.** Again and again, I saw that entrepreneurs who could craft a compelling narrative gained traction faster than those who relied solely on the strength of their products or services. Across industries, the pattern was clear: facts and features might inform, but stories engage, persuade, and ultimately drive success.

After analyzing all the conversations I've had with entrepreneurs during my podcast, several clear patterns emerged that might be helpful for your own journey:

1. **Authentic Connection is Essential.** The most successful founders established genuine connections between their personal experiences and market needs. This authenticity came through in their marketing, which resonated deeply with their target audiences.

2. **Storytelling Drives Marketing Success.** Regardless of your industry or business model, the ability to clearly communicate your *why* through compelling storytelling consistently ranked among the most critical factors of success.

3. **Multiple Paths Lead to Success.** Some businesses thrived with external funding, others by bootstrapping. Some launched quickly, others took years to develop. The common factor wasn't the specific approach, but rather the alignment between approach and vision.

4. **Relationships Matter More Than You Think.** Nearly every success story included a pivotal relationship—with a mentor, customer, investor, or partner—that opened doors or provided crucial guidance at a critical moment.

5. **Adaptability Trumps Perfect Planning.** The entrepreneurs who thrived weren't those with the most detailed initial business plans, but rather those who could adapt quickly to changing circumstances.

The Customer-Market Fit Challenge

Every successful founder I spoke with had a sharp eye for identifying gaps in the market—problems that were either ignored, underserved, or handled inefficiently. What set them apart wasn't just their ability to spot these gaps—it was how they positioned their solutions with precision. Instead of trying to be everything to everyone, they homed in on a single, high-impact issue and executed it masterfully.

One of the first steps to scaling a business is nailing your *customer-market fit*: aligning everything—your product, content, and marketing—with what your target market truly wants and values. It's not enough to have an incredible product or service. You need to ensure it solves a real problem for your target audience. This requires listening to your target audience, testing your ideas, and iterating your marketing plan continuously.

Nailing your customer-market fit typically starts right at launch, so marketing plays a critical role here—it's the vehicle through which you discover what resonates with your customers. Think of it as a constant feedback loop, where each campaign, each piece of content, and each data point informs your next move. Remember, perfecting your customer-market fit isn't a one-and-done process. It's an ongoing journey. Some things will work, and others won't. The key is to remain curious and open to learning.

The 3P Framework: The Way Forward

Looking back on my own career, I've come to appreciate the winding road that led me here. I didn't always have a plan, and for a long time, I just went with the flow. It wasn't until I hit a low point in my career that I realized I needed clarity and direction. Meditation, grit, and time—including eight transformative years in New York City—helped me find my purpose.

Entrepreneurship, much like life, is about growth and adaptation. What's clear is that entrepreneurship isn't a one-size-fits-all journey, but rather a deeply personal expression of how each founder chooses to create value in the world. My journey taught me that every step, whether planned or not, builds on the last. From my early days as a graphic designer to my transition into marketing strategy, each experience shaped my perspective. I learned to embrace both the creative and analytical sides of business, and I discovered that marketing—at its core—is about making connections that matter.

It was from these experiences and connections that I developed my practical approach to marketing: the 3Ps—Prepare, Propel, and Perfect. This framework breaks down the complexities of marketing into clear, actionable steps: laying your foundation, mapping and planning your outreach, and executing and refining. What is unique about this framework is that it views marketing not as a linear process, but as a cyclical one, where each phase supports the others and can be revisited as needed to fuel ongoing growth through both the services and the company's life.

While these phases remain consistent across industries, the key differentiator is your target audience. Your target audience isn't just who you reach or how many people—it's about deeply understanding their challenges, frustrations, and aspirations. By genuinely connecting with their needs and speaking their language, you can show how your solution fills the gaps they've been struggling with.

There's a common misconception that each industry demands entirely tailored marketing. The truth is, marketing tactics don't differ drastically from one industry to another. The real power comes from understanding the audience within that industry—getting inside their headspace, identifying their needs, and showing them how your business can be a tool that drives their success.

Great leaders aren't just visionaries—they're collaborators, listeners, and learners. As you read this book, my goal is to arm you with the tools, knowledge, and confidence to tackle marketing head-on. My 3P framework has aided countless businesses in not just saving money on ineffective marketing but in setting up strategies that genuinely foster growth and connect them to their target audience. So you can benefit from this strategy, I'm going to first walk you through what the 3P framework is on a high level, giving you some broad strokes of the marketing cycle. Let me warn you: Chapter 2 is dense, but it sets the strong foundation you'll need to master the phases. When we do go into detail in Chapters 3, 4, and 5, we'll be repeating some of the information from Chapter 2 while diving deeper into each phase's strengths and nuances. This is what marketing is: a repeated cycle, made stronger and better through constant examination of how your target audience is responding to your marketing and products. In understanding and using the 3Ps, you'll be setting yourself and your team up for success by having a marketing plan that inherently requires introspection, ongoing self-awareness, and a willingness to grow, whether you've been in business for fifteen years or haven't launched yet.

Are you ready? Let's get started.

CHAPTER 2

THE MARKETING CYCLE: A NEW APPROACH

Discipline does not mean control. Discipline means having the sense to do exactly what is needed.

– Sadh Guru, author of Inner Engineering

Marketing is often portrayed as a straightforward journey: start here, end there, and success will follow. But that's not how real businesses operate, and it's certainly not how marketing works. Marketing is not linear. It's dynamic, ever-changing, and adaptable to where you are in your business journey, to market shifts, and to your customers' evolving needs and wants. That's why I've developed a new approach based on three distinct but interconnected phases of the marketing cycle, which I call "The Three Phases of the Marketing Cycle" or the 3Ps, as you've been introduced to them. Now, you'll get to know them a bit better.

What sets my framework apart from other marketing methods is its flexibility. The three phases aren't rigid steps you check off. They're fluid, allowing you to move between them as your business evolves. Whether you're just starting out, scaling up, or pivoting in response to new challenges, this cyclical approach ensures you're always grounded in what matters most—your goals, your audience, and your ability to adapt. An effective marketing strategy isn't about complexity. It's about clarity. The marketing cycle simplifies what can often feel overwhelming, breaking down how to promote your business into actionable, repeatable steps that fit your unique needs. By embracing the 3P approach, you gain the freedom to refine, iterate, and innovate without losing sight of the bigger picture.

First, I'll walk you through the three phases of the marketing cycle, outlining how this adaptable framework can transform the way you approach growth for your business. In later chapters, we'll talk about each phase's particulars. These phases, and marketing as a whole, are not just about strategies. They're about building a sustainable foundation for your business, one phase at a time.

Marketing Requires Good Bones

You've probably heard the classic tune *Dem Bones*, the one that reminds us, "the hip bone's connected to the thigh bone." While it may seem like a simple children's rhyme, it actually serves as a powerful metaphor for marketing. Just like those bones, every element of your marketing strategy is interconnected, working together to create a strong, functional, and cohesive skeleton we can rely on. In our world, these "bones" are marketing strategies, marketing channels, and data metrics, all seamlessly connected to make up the anatomy of a well-oiled marketing machine.

While many perceive marketing as a maze of complexities—akin to solving the Rubik's cube—it's not that complicated, at least not when you have a guide to help you. At its core, marketing is a form of relationship science, an ongoing conversation between you and your audience—one that never ends as long as you are in business. This is why it's critical not to stop marketing, no matter what stage you're in.

Businesses naturally go through cycles—highs, lows, and moments of uncertainty. And while it's smart to scale back during challenging times, it's even smarter to focus your efforts on the channels that drive real ROI, not just the "nice-to-haves." Consistency is what keeps the conversation—and your business—alive. No one wants to relive the uncertainty of the COVID days, where businesses and opportunities available to customers were constantly in flux. The companies that kept marketing and pivoted their offerings to fit their target audiences' needs during these uncertain times were the ones that thrived, while a lot of their competitors who pulled back didn't make it. That's exactly why you can't stop marketing, even when things get tough. The COVID years are also a reminder that being flexible—adapting to whatever gets thrown at you—is the key to staying in the game and coming out stronger. The idea is not to cut marketing entirely, but to scale back and focus on things that have a true ROI rather than nice-to-haves.

Let's face it—social media platforms are great, but the wild thing is they take up more time than any other marketing channel. For some companies, social media is revenue-driving, but for others it can be a nice-to-have. So what I mean is, if social media falls into being a nice-to-have for you, but you know that the marketing efforts that really drive your ROI aren't social media, you don't need to be posting twelve times a week. Scale back to three times, if needed.

The truth is, most of us are looking at marketing the wrong way. It's an investment, not a line item. This is a shift most companies need to make, all the way up to the corporate level. Instead of wading through a labyrinth of buzzwords and jargon, following what's trending, or doing everything that's presented to you, you need to find out what keeps the line of communication open between you and your target audience.

I'm inviting you to a refreshingly straightforward outlook on marketing. Not just one segment of it, but the whole gamut. I've peeled back the layers to reveal the interconnected 'bones' that underpin every successful marketing venture. Together, we'll traverse this landscape step-by-step, much like that old tune takes you from one bone to the next.

Don't get me wrong, there are some nuances to marketing beyond what I go over in here, and I don't mean to trivialize them. But this book isn't about the specifics—it's about the foundational elements to successful, purpose-filled, audience-connecting marketing. That's what I aim to break down. Understanding the process and the bigger picture will allow for a smoother ride into your business's growth, versus having to step back and build the foundation when you are already launched. Believe me, a lot of companies make this mistake, and the biggest one is skipping out on foundational work.

Imagine a world in which you set something up right from the beginning, versus having to spend more time and effort later down the road. I witness the latter every day. Except we don't get to stop in our tracks to fix this first before continuing. We have to work through it as the business is still going. Building it right from the beginning will save you money in the long run.

This is why I'm making it as easy to understand as a childhood jingle, to help simplify it all. With this approach, you'll see how these marketing bones connect, allowing you to move effortlessly from strategy to execution, much like how walking requires each bone in your leg to function in harmony. In a similar fashion, all the pieces for marketing need to fit together to form a smoother growth and build a strong skeleton you can rely on.

The Cyclical Approach

Picture it like this: envision your business as a giant cogwheel, segmented into three significant phases, each representing a cycle. Every time we accomplish a milestone in one segment, the entire cogwheel turns, enabling the next section to align with our laser focus. This rotational mechanism ensures that we're not just putting out fires or chasing after the next shiny object. We're systematically building a resilient, scalable, and indeed, brilliant marketing machine. It's crucial to understand how each flows into the next and cycles back with one another, creating a perpetual loop of optimization. This allows us to uncover gaps and inject growth. Don't fret if you have been in business for a long time and you need to take a step back to see what's what— what's working for you and what isn't. We can use these phases to fine-tune the engine you already have.

It doesn't matter whether you're in the fragile infancy stages of a startup, still sorting out your Minimum Viable Product (MVP), a product with just enough features to satisfy early customers and provide feedback for future product development (you don't need to be at 100 percent when you're in the testing phase), or whether you're steering the ship of an established, soon to be *Fortune* 500 behemoth, you should always be evaluating your growth. The key brilliance of these cycles is that they adapt and will never stop, no matter how small or how big you get. These aren't ephemeral trends or flavor-of-the-month tactics. These are fundamental principles that transcend industry, scale, and even time.

My signature, time-tested, battle-hardened methodology, "The Three Phases of the Marketing Cycle," the 3Ps, is the magnum opus of my professional journey, born from years in the trenches, periods of sheer exhilaration, and yes, moments of despair. The elements of these cycles are not new. However, the way I'm bundling them together is. All to help you understand how to approach them from start to finish, or rather, from start to ongoing cycle.

When a client walks into my world—be it a cluttered garage startup or a sprawling corporate campus—we don't start our talk with numbers. Obviously, that is the end goal, but the first thing we do is sit down and go over the 3Ps, my whys to this approach, how we will tackle them, and most importantly, alignment. Don't get me wrong, the goal settings are where the numbers come in and what make your business's heartbeat keep moving, and those are all great, but to get there, we have to establish the foundation and the core strength of the business. Otherwise, you have a product or service that no one resonates with, as brilliant as it may be, and those numbers won't ever be reached.

You see, the 3Ps aren't just theoretical constructs or nebulous concepts to scribble on a whiteboard and forget. No, they're actionable frameworks. When I guide my clients through each phase, it's like watching a fog lift from a landscape. Suddenly, everything is vivid, the path is clear, and most notably, the horizon is within reach. That, my friends, is what I live for—the *aha* moment that transforms ambiguity into clarity, hesitation into decisiveness. But let's get one thing straight: adopting the 3Ps isn't a quick fix or a one-and-done deal. It's akin to a company's core lifestyle change— it's habitual, a commitment to the perpetual pursuit of marketing excellence.

In today's volatile, fast-paced business ecosystem, "good enough" simply isn't. Yes, there is the get-to-market-at-80-percent rule, rather than delaying and never getting to market. However, that 80 percent needs to be almost perfect. You need to be brilliant, and brilliance doesn't have an expiration date. So, whether you're about to embark on your first entrepreneurial venture, or you're looking to inject a newfound sense of vitality into an age-old enterprise or remix your tactics in a younger startup, remember that the 3Ps aren't just the crown jewel of my practice. It's the royal road to sustainable, scalable, and remarkable marketing success.

Now, let's get this machine up and running with a high-level overview of the marketing cycle phases.

Phase One: Prepare

What's the cornerstone of any grand edifice? You got it—a sturdy foundation. In the business realm, this translates to understanding the inner architecture of your brand. Prepare isn't the get-to-it-later phase. This is the drop-everything-and-focus phase. This is where you get intimate with your objectives, align them with your vision, and breathe life into what I am calling the 4Ws.

Originally, Author Simon Sinek in *Start with Why* referred to what he called the Golden Circle. Made up of *why*, *how*, and *what*, Sinek's Golden Circle creates an outward-moving plan to inspire the people in your company and to get people to buy your company's product. I've modified and expanded on his idea to include what is most important in building your content to find and inspire your target audience. I call this the 4Ws, and they are:

Why: The purpose or belief behind your product or service—why you do what you do.

What: Your product or services offered.

Way: Your unique process—the way you do it.

Who: The target and specific audiences who would benefit from it.

If your company were a person, what would it say, how would it behave, what would it stand for? Since we are on this path, how would it even sound? Is it rock 'n' roll, or classical music, or '90s hip-hop? You get where I am going.

Basically, the 4Ws are the makeup of your brand. These aren't just existential questions. They're business imperatives, ultimately your business's journey. Do not skimp on your *who*—your target audiences; we're talking knowing in deep-level who your customers are, not superficial sketches of them. Like you, you don't have just one segment of an audience. Who are they, what do they care about, what are their needs? But don't fall into the trap of thinking you are the audience. You may have built this out of frustration or a gap in the market, but now's the time to take yourself out of the equation and get deep with the audience outside of yourself that you are serving.

One of the biggest pitfalls we see in marketing is that businesses often completely skip this foundation-building phase. This oversight becomes detrimental when they later encounter roadblocks and struggle to understand why their initiatives aren't moving forward. This step is crucial to avoid constant backtracking and re-optimizing for growth. In my experience working with clients, especially established businesses puzzled by their inability to reach goals, this foundational phase is precisely where we begin—because understanding your brand architecture is not optional, it's essential for sustainable success.

Phase Two: Propel

Now that the stage is set, let's roll up our sleeves and plunge into Phase Two. This is where strategy takes center stage and you propel your marketing efforts into action. How do you expect to meet, let alone exceed, your quarterly or yearly targets without a road map? How will you recognize growth if you don't define what it looks like? We'll be drafting blueprints and key performance indicators (KPIs)—data metrics that you set up to assign responsibilities and achieve your targets.

This phase is like when the pieces of a well-oiled machine move in perfect harmony toward a shared vision. Is your website up to snuff? Does it articulate your brand's narrative? What I mean is if you sell bikes, tell your customers you sell bikes, not the breeze that blows through their hair. Your martech stack—which is your marketing technology stack of tools—connects every detail and aspect of your business, allowing you to track a signup from your website all the way to a sale and everything in between. Essentially, your martech stack allows you to follow your customer on their journey from discovery to sale. It should be more than just a collection of software. It needs to be an interconnected ecosystem ready to capture, analyze, and interpret data from every conceivable touchpoint, and believe me, you don't need many.

Phase Three: Perfect

At the start, when you lack data, you'll need to make decisions without knowing their outcomes, which is fine. This initial step is about building your datasets and understanding what works and what doesn't. But now, we have the pièce de résistance: Phase Three.

After all the work you've done in Phase One and in Phase Two, now in Phase Three, you begin to perfect your strategy by knowing how to interpret what is working and what isn't. The process is testing your marketing strategy and refining it to empower you in the moves you make.

Imagine having a crystal ball that tells you exactly how to outmaneuver your competition— maybe with AI today, it will do just that! Well, for now, data analytics is that crystal ball. What you have collected from your martech stack becomes your direction of plays, your strategic maneuvers of metrics that translate into actionable insights. You're no longer reacting; you're predicting and making moves based on data. You're not just playing the game anymore; you're changing it.

To Sum It All Up

Phase One *prepares* you and gets you ready, Phase Two *propels* you and sets you on course, and Phase Three helps you *perfect* your strategy in a way that keeps you in perpetual motion as the machine keeps moving.

As you get your feet wet in this ocean of opportunities, remember this: The marketing cycle never stops. It's an ever-revolving wheel of refinement. Adding a new product? Back to Phase One. Witnessed a seasonal dip? Revisit Phases Two and Three. Is your messaging all convoluted? Review Phase One. Data showing a new trend? Phases Two and Three beckon.

What you're doing here, right now, is so much more than just reading a book—you're embarking on a journey that will transform how you run your business and connect with your audience. This journey will help you save thousands, maybe even millions, in marketing costs while mastering the fundamentals that drive real results. By the end, you'll be equipped to work alongside marketing professionals as a knowledgeable partner, not just a client.

As outlined on the next page, Figure 2.1 showcases the three main cycles of marketing, and the details of each cycle are described in Figure 2.2. We will dig deeper into the details of each phase and why they matter in the following chapters.

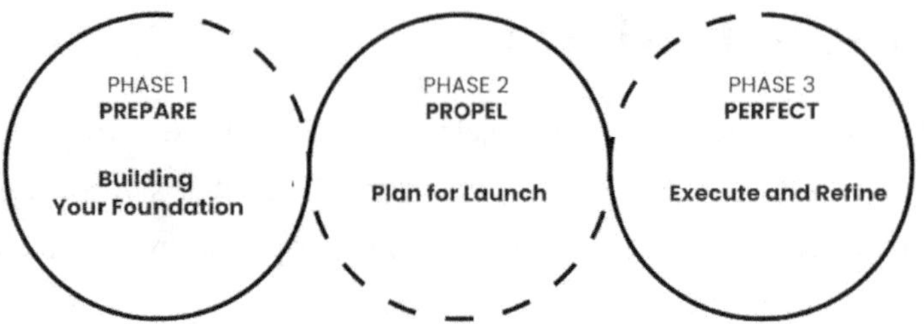

Figure 2.1: Three Phases of Marketing

PHASE 1

PREPARE

Building Your Foundation: In this phase, we establish the essential elements of your marketing foundation.

- Company Objectives
- Budget
- The 4 W's Framework
- Target Customer Profile

PHASE 2

PROPEL

Plan for Launch: With your foundation set, we now focus on creating the systems and strategy to reach your market.

- Website Optimization
- Marketing Tools Stack:
- Go-to-Market Strategy

PHASE 3

PERFECT

Execute and Refine: Focus on action, data-driven refinement, and scaling for growth.

- Content Creation and Distribution
- Channel Optimization
- Performance Tracking
- Iteration and Scaling

Figure 2.2: Phases of Marketing Details

Simple as that, right? But before we get deeper into the 3Ps, let's explore an important and often overlooked aspect of the marketing landscape: the customer journey. It's intimately intertwined with the 3Ps, essentially forming two journeys that share one path.

The Customer Journey: Two Journeys, One Path

The customer's journey has evolved far beyond the simple linear path to purchase we once knew. Today, it's an intricate dance between your business's evolution and your customer's experience—a relationship that weaves through every phase of your marketing strategy. While many businesses focus solely on moving customers through a sales funnel, the real magic happens when you understand how your business journey parallels and supports your customer's journey through each stage of growth. Think of it as a double helix, where your business journey and customer journey spiral together, each strengthening the other because they need one another to survive.

As Russell Brunson, founder of ClickFunnels, demonstrated when he launched his platform in 2014, an effective customer journey isn't just about pushing people through a funnel—it's about creating a seamless experience that guides customers naturally toward solutions. After struggling with his own early online ventures and learning marketing through trial and error, Brunson recognized that businesses needed tools to help people make money from home without investing any web development skills. Brunson became obsessed with sales funnels—the step-by-step process that guides potential customers from initial interest to final purchase. So he built a system that transformed how entrepreneurs approach their marketing strategy: ClickFunnels, a drag-and-drop platform that democratized what was once the domain of expensive web developers and marketing agencies. This system transformed how entrepreneurs approach their marketing strategy, shifting focus from building websites to creating conversion-focused funnels that actually sell products and services.

Figure 2.3: Three Ps Marketing Funnel

Understanding this comprehensive journey is crucial for businesses seeking sustainable growth, as it reveals valuable touchpoints for building stronger relationships, identifies opportunities to reduce friction, increases customer retention, and ultimately transforms satisfied customers into brand advocates who drive organic acquisition through word-of-mouth. I first saw this in action while supporting a healthcare and wellness provider, where mapping the full client journey—from initial inquiry to ongoing care—allowed us to identify where trust was breaking down and where stronger engagement could be built. The lessons from that experience helped shape my 3P system, and what I found is that these principles apply far beyond healthcare. Whether in industries like tech, professional services, and consumer goods, mastering the customer journey isn't optional—it's the foundation for turning one-time buyers into loyal advocates who fuel sustainable growth. Of course, every customer or client journey is unique to your business, industry, and offering, which is why it's critical to tailor your approach to the specific needs, wants, and desires of your audience.

Aligning the 3Ps and the Customer Journey

The true power of the 3P framework lies in its seamless alignment with your customer's journey, creating a synchronized path where business development and customer experience evolve together.

Here's how aligning the customer journey with the 3P framework works:

Phase One: Prepare. As you lay down your foundation, you're creating the environment for customer discovery: generating awareness and grabbing their interest. Keep in mind, *awareness* means they are just getting to know you. *Interest* means they are beginning to dig further, comparing you to your potential competitors and determining how you could benefit them.

Phase Two: Propel. Through strategic mapping, you're touching every point in your customers' journey from consideration and evaluation, leading them into a purchase *decision*, which is the ultimate *action* you want them to take, before eventually leading them into a post-purchase and loyalty environment.

Phase Three: Perfect. As you sharpen and optimize your approach, you're evolving with your customers' needs, which feeds into the entire customer journey from discovery to loyalty.

Gone are the days of linear progression from awareness to consideration to purchase. Your potential customers might discover you through an ever-growing, interconnected web of touchpoints. This circular discovery process means your marketing plan must be strategically thought through to capture and nurture these various touchpoints, creating a cohesive experience regardless of how customers find you and purchase from you.

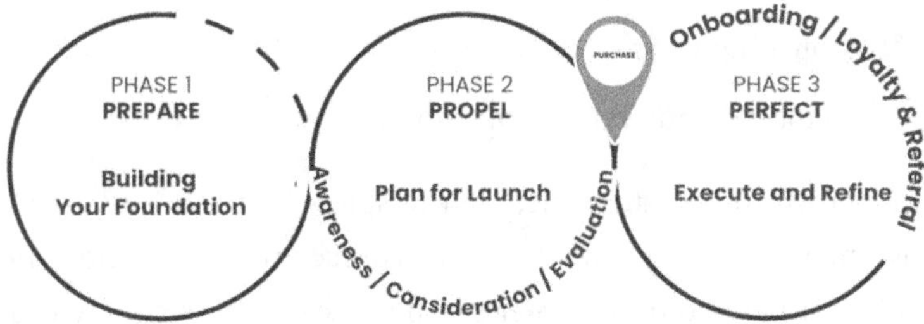

Figure 2.4: The Point of Purchase

Now that you get the 3Ps from a high-level, let's get a little cozier and detailed with these concepts as they relate to your customers.

Phase One: Prepare for Customer Discovery

Your business journey begins with a critical first step: creating the foundation for customer discovery. Phase One directly aligns with the customer journey's Discovery and Awareness Stage, where potential customers first encounter your brand.

While establishing your *why* (purpose), *what* (offering), *way* (methods), and *who* (audience), you're simultaneously creating the entry points for customer discovery. This isn't just about business planning; it's about crafting the environment where initial customer interactions can begin and thrive.

The process involves

- Identifying market gaps.

- Understanding and segmenting buyer personas.

- Addressing unique customer pain points—a problem or frustration that a customer has and wants a solution for.

- Defining your brand's distinctive personality.

- Establishing KPIs.

- Developing your value proposition.

Know this: In this storyline, your business isn't the hero—your customer is. Your product or service becomes the armor and tools that help your customer reach success. You're simply providing what they need to achieve their own victories.

Phase Two: Propel to Shape Customers' Path to Purchase

Phase Two is where strategy takes center stage and your marketing outreach expands into the circular discovery phase. Directly aligned with two stages of the customer journey, the Consideration and Evaluation Stage and the Purchase Decision Stage, Phase Two is where your comprehensive marketing plan comes to life. How do you expect to meet, let alone exceed, your quarterly and yearly targets without a comprehensive plan? This roadmap will help you guide potential customers through these stages, which are critical decision-making moments for customers.

For the Consideration and Evaluation Stage, you should:

- Craft content that helps customers research and compare options

- Create engaging materials that showcase your unique value proposition

- Develop resources that address potential customer questions and concerns

- Establish credibility through thought leadership and transparent communication

For the Purchase Decision Stage, you should

- Design intuitive paths to purchase

- Create compelling calls-to-action

- Streamline the transaction experience

- Provide clear, supportive guidance through the buying process

In Phase Two, your martech stack becomes crucial—it's not just a collection of tools but an interconnected ecosystem ready to capture, analyze, and interpret data from every conceivable touchpoint.

Think of Phase One as pre-party planning: It's critical, and the bulk of activity occurs there. But Phase Two is the party itself, bustling with guests, conversations, and interactions. Your marketing plan orchestrates this party—determining which channels to use, what content to create, how to engage different audience segments, and when to deploy various party tactics. Remember to keep it simple. Continuously test to know what is working and learn what isn't.

Phase Three: Perfect by Driving Customer Loyalty and Retention

Here's where the real magic of alignment happens. After all the work done in the previous phases, understanding what is working and what isn't in Phase One and Phase Two, Phase Three becomes your center for interpreting results—empowering every move you make from here on out.

This phase is vital for understanding and enhancing the customer's post-purchase experience, driving loyalty and retention. It goes beyond the transaction. Instead, the initial post-purchase considerations focus on

- Smooth onboarding processes.

- Welcome communication.

- Early to immediate post-purchase engagement strategies.

- Setting expectations for future interactions.

Each element of your business's growth directly enhances customer experiences. The more growth you have and the more you know about what your customers like and dislike about your existing systems, the more you're prepared to give them better experiences on repeat. Such improvements you can make to improve customer experience can be

- Refined messaging that leads to more relevant communications

- Optimized website that creates a more intuitive journey

- Improving marketing funnels to create smoother paths to continued engagement

- Enhanced customer service processes, which build stronger loyalty

- Upgrading tech stack, enabling a more personalized experience.

The beauty of Phase Three is that it never truly ends. Each improvement in your business operations translates directly into enhanced customer journeys, creating a virtuous cycle—not a vicious one!—where business growth and customer satisfaction feed into each other.

Tailoring the Journey to Your Business Model

It is important to identify your business model, B2C or B2B, in preparation for all that you build throughout your marketing journey, as the sales cycle of these will be distinctly different. In a B2C (Business-to-Consumer) Journey, you should

- Focus on emotional connection and personal transformation

- Help customers see themselves as heroes in their own narrative

- Support specific content types: blog posts, social media updates, product stories, testimonials

- Have the goal of bridging the gap between who customers are and who they want to become

In a B2B (Business-to-Business) Journey, you should

- Emphasize clarity, precision, and tangible business value

- Demonstrate concrete solutions and ROI

- Support specific content types: whitepapers, case studies, implementation guides

- Have the goal of providing actionable insights that drive business growth

Essential Elements for an Effective Customer Journey

Creating an effective customer journey isn't just about having good customer service—it's about building a system that actually works and satisfies your customer. These elements aren't nice-to-haves. They're the foundation that separates companies that truly connect with their customers from those that are just going through the motions. But you might be wondering, what are the elements that a B2C or B2B needs to satisfy its customers? Here's a quick list:

Foundational Elements

- **Active Listening**: Create multiple channels for customers to share feedback

- **Pain Point Precision**: Address specific challenges with custom-designed solutions

- **Corporate Social Responsibility**: Take meaningful action on larger societal issues

Personalization Elements

- **Customization**: Create experiences attuned to individual needs

- **Behavioral Personalization**: Use past interactions to predict future needs

- **Contextual Adaptation**: Adjust experiences based on real-time situations

- **Relationship Management**: Build meaningful, long-term connections

Technical Elements

- **Omnichannel Integration**: Create seamless experiences across all platforms

- **Technology Enablers**: Utilize AI, machine learning, and analytics

- **Data Analytics**: Convert customer interactions into actionable insights

- **Feedback Loops**: Create ongoing dialogues that shape experiences

Wrapping It All Up

As we've mapped the intricate dance between business strategy through the 3P cycle and customer experience, a powerful narrative emerges: The real magic lies in recognizing that your business journey and your customers' journeys are not separate paths, but a single, spiraling narrative of mutual discovery and growth. From the initial spark of awareness to the depths of loyalty, a strategic, adaptive approach can transform traditional marketing into a responsive, collaborative ecosystem.

The customer journey is no longer a linear path but a throughline that continues to be the foundation for a dynamic, interconnected circular process where every business decision directly shapes and enhances customer interactions. Today, marketing is about more than just tactics or touchpoints—it's about creating a living, breathing relationship between a business and its customers. Each phase of the 3P framework—Prepare, Propel, and Perfect—isn't just a stage in business development, but rather a critical opportunity to understand, engage, and grow with your audience.

Like any relationship in life, the connection between company and customer is constantly evolving. Here is the reality: With all the options out there, as entrepreneurs and business owners, we can't just "set it and forget it" anymore. We need to keep growing, adapting, and responding to how our audience feels, because they, in essence, dictate the market's purchasing power.

I'm sure you are asking how, exactly, do we prepare for the best launch? How do we propel forward when we've already have a good thing going? Is perfection even attainable if we need to keep growing and changing? Let me tell you this: It is possible. As we jump into the details of the 3Ps in the next three chapters, you'll see exactly how each phase synchronizes with the customer, and how you can use them as flexible tools that will become your sustainable marketing plan and sync with your customer at every stage, giving your company a stable foundation to grow from.

Now that you're a bit better *prepared* to learn the nitty-gritty of the 3Ps, let's jump into Phase One: Prepare!

CHAPTER 3

PHASE ONE: PREPARE

Put Down a Rock-Solid Foundation

A goal without a plan is just a wish.
– Antoine de Saint-Exupéry

Phase One is pivotal in the cyclical nature of marketing—something we've already explored and touched upon, but will now go deeper into. In this phase, we establish the essential elements of your marketing foundation.

Whether you're just starting your marketing journey or have been in business for years, you will either begin at Phase One or revisit it to strengthen your foundational strategies. This is especially true when introducing a new product or service. Knowing when, how, and where this phase fits into your broader goals is key to setting yourself up for success.

Phase One ensures your business's foundation is rock solid—a stable launchpad for all your marketing efforts. Before you move forward, you need to establish four critical building blocks. These include:

- Aligning with your company objectives
- Defining your budget
- Establishing your brand's 4W framework
- Crafting a detailed customer profile

Many businesses overlook the importance of truly understanding their audience, but this step is essential to creating marketing strategies that resonate and deliver results. What I mean by overlook is that they understand the high level of who their audience is, but they aren't going deeper.

What's great about where we are today is the age of our AI explosion (I say explosion because AI has been around for many years, but we're in a gold rush of new AI companies, and they just keep growing). Today, with the presence of large language models like ChatGPT, we've been blessed with speed and agility to market. One barrier that I strongly believe deters many entrepreneurs from entering business is getting the foundational build-out done because it actually requires work. Efforts and research cost a pretty penny, and if not a penny to pay someone else, you're paying with your time and energy, which is probably two shiny pennies! These fundamentals take a lot of time, but now we have tools to get this done faster.

My point is that these tools can help with research and strategies, making it easier to build your foundation. Then you can run them by a marketing expert to ensure you're on the right path. Remember, these tools are not perfect. They can still make mistakes. They're learning and ever-evolving, but they're an excellent jumping-off point for you to begin this phase. (If you're not using these tools, get on it—ride this wave and don't fall behind, because who knows, our whole lives might be automated very soon.)

At the core of Phase One is what you've already been introduced to, the 4Ws: Why, What, Way, and Who. These serve as a reference for refining your brand messaging and market positioning. *Why* does your business exist? *What* unique value do you offer? In what *way* can you connect with your audience most effectively? And *who* is your ideal customer? Answering these questions builds a clear, actionable roadmap for your marketing efforts.

Even if you're a company that's been running marketing efforts for years, you might find yourself hitting a plateau. When marketing stops supporting your growth, it's time to circle back to Phase One. In this case, Phase One becomes an audit—a chance to evaluate your current strategies and pinpoint adjustments to get back on track. It's an opportunity to revisit your foundational elements to ensure they're still aligned with your goals and the needs of your audience.

Revisiting Phase One isn't just a one-time event. It's something that, as time goes on and you're using the 3Ps, you'll instinctively know to do as markets shift and your audience evolves. This ensures your messaging remains relevant, aligned with current trends, and capable of cutting through the noise to connect with your customers. Auditing keeps your business in sync with the market, allowing you to stay ahead of competitors and maintain momentum. In short, Phase One is your opportunity to get organized, stay relevant, and create a sturdy base that empowers all your marketing efforts moving forward. Let's start with aligning your company's objectives with your business goals.

Company Objectives: Aligning Marketing with Business Goals

Every foundational element ties back to your company's objectives. One of the first steps in Phase One of the marketing cycle is defining these objectives based on your offerings. When many people think of objectives, their first instinct is sales. If you're just starting out, it's crucial to establish clear sales goals for both the quarterly and annual periods. For established businesses, revisiting these goals is equally important—especially when launching new products or services or shifting marketing efforts. In fact, this is a process you'll repeat year after year to ensure you're consistently aligned with your growth aspirations.

Let me give you some examples of how this works. Say you're launching a B2C product, like an adaptive lighting lamp that adjusts brightness based on room conditions for optimal photography. Your objectives might include capturing 5 percent market share in the home photography equipment space within twelve months, building brand awareness among content creators aged twenty-five to forty, and achieving $500,000 in direct-to-consumer sales through your website and Amazon.

For a B2B example, imagine you're offering project management software for construction companies. Your objectives could be securing fifty mid-sized construction firms as clients in year one, establishing partnerships with three major industry associations, and generating $2 million in annual recurring revenue while maintaining a 90 percent customer retention rate.

Setting company objectives isn't just about tracking numbers. It's about creating a roadmap that informs every decision you make as a business owner and marketer by giving you a goal to reach. By analyzing your company's portfolio of services and products, you can better understand the strategies required to achieve your sales targets. This clarity also enables you to determine budget allocations and estimate the cost per acquisition (CPA) for new customers—which is your marketing efforts' cost to bring in a new customer—ensuring that your marketing efforts remain efficient and effective.

Managing Acquisition Costs

Let me tell you about a startup I worked with that offered free sample boxes of products. We faced a unique challenge: managing customer acquisition costs for a platform that was entirely free. Customers signed up to receive monthly gift boxes tailored to their profiles and product preferences. The signup process included a detailed form to gather data, which allowed us to hyper-target products from our consumer-packaged goods (CPG) partners to the right audience.

We made money through our partnerships, so this approach not only elevated the customers' experiences but also provided valuable insights to our partners about their ideal customer profiles, as we were able to hyper-target and get their products in the hands of the exact customers they were looking for.

Since the platform was free, profitability hinged on meticulous calculations. We focused on customer lifetime value (CLV), a critical metric that reflects the total worth of a customer over their relationship with the business, starting from the initial purchase. CLV is calculated by multiplying the average value of a purchase, the number of purchases per year, and the average length of the customer relationship.

With these metrics, we determined that our acquisition cost per member needed to stay at $0.75 or less. This experience offered invaluable lessons about balancing cost per lead (CPL)—the cost of generating one potential customer—and overall marketing efforts to maintain profitability.

To avoid confusion, note that since this was free for each member, we had to perform back-of-the-napkin calculations on the cost per box, factoring in that each member received one box per month with an average number of samples inside, based on the CPG companies with which we were working. So, it's a little different and nuanced in this situation, which is very rare—hence why I wanted to bring it up.

In another case, while I worked for an enterprise media company under the scrutiny of the world's microscope, we engaged a large consulting company that assisted with our business objectives to expand revenue streams for the company. Granted (and this is key to remember), just because you hire an external company that will do months on end of research to come up with suggestions to help you build additional products and services, they may not always win in the market. Some may fall flat, and some may last only a couple of months. That's why it's vital to be open to testing. Everyone goes through this, from startups all the way up to enterprise.

Learning from our failures was crucial to the successes we had moving forward, as we transformed our mistakes into improved services and products tailored to the needs of our clients. You are never too big or too small to recognize bumps along the way, so why not take a step back, be proud of the accomplishments, then fine-tune your approach, making it that much more efficient?

From Objectives to Key Performance Indicators

Understanding your objectives enables you to identify the right KPIs to track progress. For acquisition-focused goals, metrics like cost per lead, conversion rates, and website traffic become essential tracking points. For retention objectives, look at repeat purchase rates, customer satisfaction scores, and churn—when customers cancel subscriptions, stop making purchases, or abandon your product and or service entirely. These indicators serve as early warning signs, allowing you to adjust strategies before they impact your bottom line.

Creating Cross-Functional Alignment

Effective objectives don't exist in a marketing vacuum—they require buy-in across departments, even if your departments are small and you are just starting off. Understanding these parameters doesn't just guide marketing strategies—it also fosters clear communication across teams. When sales can align seamlessly with marketing goals, it creates a unified approach to engaging potential clients. Financially, knowing your objectives helps evaluate the feasibility of campaigns based on budgets and expected returns. It aligns product development with marketing promotions, ensuring your customer service team understands acquisition goals that might increase support requests. When everyone works toward shared objectives, resources are allocated more efficiently and customer experiences become more consistent. I'm encouraging you to think big picture in Phase One, for future setup and growth. Remember: Failure isn't an option. By regularly revisiting and adjusting these objectives, businesses can remain agile, adapting to market shifts and evolving based on customer behaviors. This iterative process ensures sustained growth, profitability, and a competitive edge in an ever-changing business landscape. Your company objectives are more than just a checklist—they're the cornerstone of your success.

Set Measurable Sales Goals

Let's take Phase One a step further: start defining your objectives now by breaking them into actionable, measurable goals. Use the provided section below to map out your sales targets, align them with your broader vision, and ensure they reflect the needs of your audience and the growth you're striving for.

Understand Your Business Goals

Identify the primary goals of your business, whether it's increasing revenue, acquiring new customers, retaining existing ones, expanding market reach, or launching new products or services. Ensure these goals are realistic and aligned with the core value your business provides to its customers, whether individuals (B2C) or other businesses (B2B).

Additionally, what is the broader purpose of your business? Sure, you're in it for the profit, but what about the impact your product or service has on society? Aligning your business goals with your company's social responsibility can not only add depth to your brand but also introduce new avenues for expansion. Ask yourself, "How is my business contributing to the greater good? What legacy will it leave?" Your goals should strive to answer these questions.

Transforming ambitious business goals into concrete, actionable sales targets is essential for driving growth and maintaining accountability across your organization. We can break this down even further with a chart that utilizes the four-quarter system in business. The following framework helps you establish meaningful benchmarks that align with your specific business model and industry context.

Break your sales goals into clear, measurable quarterly and annual targets. For B2C businesses, consider metrics like the number of units sold, average order value (the typical amount spent per transaction), or customer retention rates (the percentage of customers who continue to purchase from you over time). These consumer-focused metrics help you track both immediate sales performance and long-term customer value.

For B2B companies, focus on KPIs like total contract value (the complete financial worth of a client agreement), lead-to-customer conversion rates (the percentage of prospects that become paying customers), and recurring revenue (predictable income from ongoing subscriptions or service agreements). These business-oriented metrics reflect the typically longer sales cycles and higher transaction values in B2B relationships.

Time Period	Sales Target	Key Metrics
Q1		
Q2		
Q3		
Q4		
Annual Total		

Figure 3.1: Quarterly Targets

Evaluate Your Product or Service Portfolio

A strategic assessment of your offerings is crucial for optimizing your marketing resources and focusing on what truly drives business growth. This evaluation helps you identify which elements of your portfolio deserve the most investment and attention.

Assess how each product or service supports your objectives by conducting a comprehensive portfolio analysis. This involves examining performance data, customer feedback, and market trends to understand the true impact of each offering.

For B2C businesses, consider which products drive the most sales or customer loyalty. Look beyond simple revenue figures to identify products that create enthusiastic repeat customers, generate positive word-of-mouth, or serve as "gateway" purchases that lead to additional sales. Sometimes your most valuable products aren't those with the highest price tags, but those that build the strongest emotional connections with your audience.

For B2B, identify services or solutions that bring the highest value to your clients and align with their pain points or business goals. Focus on offerings that considerably improve your clients' operations, reduce their costs, or help them achieve measurable success. Solutions that address critical business challenges often command premium pricing and foster stronger client relationships, making them especially valuable within your portfolio.

Product or Service	Revenue Contribution	Growth Potential	Strategic Priority

Figure 3.2: Product or Service Evaluation Chart

Establish a Budget Framework

Creating a comprehensive budget framework forms the financial backbone of your marketing strategy, ensuring you have adequate resources to achieve your objectives while maintaining profitability. This basic framework goes beyond simply setting spending limits—it's a tool that enables growth and adaptation.

Determine the resources you'll need to support your goals, including marketing, staffing, and operational costs. Your marketing budget should account for both digital and traditional channels, content creation, advertising spending, marketing technology platforms, and analytics tools. Staffing considerations should include both internal team members and external specialists or agencies that provide expertise in specific areas. Operational costs encompass everything from customer relationship management (CRM) systems to event participation and sales enablement materials.

Keep your budget flexible to accommodate testing and adjustments as you learn what works. The most effective budget frameworks allocate 70 – 80 percent to proven strategies that reliably deliver results, while reserving 20 – 30 percent for experimentation with new approaches, channels, or audience segments. If you're just starting out and haven't tested marketing before, expect to spend a larger portion on experimentation until you identify which strategies consistently perform. This balanced approach ensures stability over time while creating space for innovation and discovery.

Budget Category	Allocation	Target Cost Per Acquisition
Marketing & Advertising	$	$
Sales Resources	$	$
Product Development	$	$
Customer Support	$	$
Operations & Technology	$	$
Personnel & Hiring	$	$
Contingency Funds	$	$

Figure 3.3: Budget Framework Chart

Build in regular review points to reallocate resources based on performance data, shifting funds from underperforming initiatives to those showing the strongest returns.

Adapt and Evolve with Market Changes

Regularly revisit your objectives and strategies based on customer feedback, market trends, and performance metrics. For example, if B2C customers are showing interest in a new product category or B2B clients are requesting a specific feature, adjust your plans to meet those demands.

Review Schedule	Key Questions to Ask	Action Items
Monthly	Are we on track with our KPIs? What tactical adjustments are needed?	
Quarterly	Which channels are performing best? Should we reallocate resources?	
Annual	How have market conditions changed? Do our objectives need revision?	

Figure 3.4: Market Change Chart

One thing I want to emphasize is celebrating failures as stepping stones, as it's an integral part of this journey. Embracing setbacks isn't about glorifying mistakes. It's about learning, iterating, and growing stronger. Each misstep offers a unique lesson, sharpening your strategy and bringing you one step closer to your goals. Failures illuminate the path ahead, revealing unseen opportunities and areas for innovation. They foster resilience and creativity, pushing you to think outside the box and approach challenges with a fresh perspective.

In a landscape where no two companies are alike, embracing the individuality of your journey, including its highs and lows, is key. It's through navigating these unique challenges and learning from misadventures that your company crafts its own narrative of success.

Your Marketing Budget: The Fuel of Any Business

Now that you understand the budgetary basics and how they align with company objectives, let's unpack the budget build-out to ensure you are fueling your business efficiently, as it has a direct impact on your go-to-market (GTM) strategy. Without understanding how much you can spend and where your priorities lie, your efforts won't reach their full potential. Think of your budget as the fuel for your GTM vehicle. You could have the flashiest car, but without enough gas—or the right kind—you won't go far, or even anywhere.

Budgeting isn't just about throwing money at tools or advertising. It's about being intentional and methodical. And remember, budgets don't have to be enormous, especially if you're just starting out. Creativity and resourcefulness are your best allies. Leverage partnerships, community outreach, and even bartering to stretch every dollar. It doesn't always have to begin with traditional ways of marketing, such as a digital campaign. Use free or low-cost methods like customer conversations, surveys, or focus groups to uncover insights. A small budget, used wisely, can deliver big results when paired with a strategic process. As I always like to say: think high impact, low cost!

Budget Allocation by Business Stage

The reality is that a startup's marketing needs are completely different from an established company's priorities. Your budget allocation should reflect your current stage and what you're trying to accomplish:

- **Startups and small businesses (pre-revenue):** Allocate 25 – 30 percent toward brand awareness, 50 percent on lead generation activities, and 20 – 25 percent for tools and infrastructure

- **Growth-stage businesses:** Shift to 15 – 20 percent for awareness, 60 percent for acquisition and conversion tactics, and 20 percent for retention strategies

- **Established businesses:** Typically allocate 10 – 15 percent for brand maintenance, 40 – 50 percent for acquisition, and 35 – 40 percent for retention and loyalty programs

Every dollar spent should be trackable and accountable. Establish clear KPIs for each marketing initiative before spending begins, as well as a clear budget reallocation framework. Here are four KPIs to keep in mind:

- Set a testing timeline for new channels (usually three to six months)

- Establish performance thresholds that trigger reallocation decisions

- Reserve 15 – 20 percent of your budget as a "pivot fund" for quick shifts to better-performing channels

- Document learnings from underperforming investments to inform future budget planning

And finally, it is important to structure your budget planning around business cycles—monthly reviews for tactical adjustments, quarterly evaluations for strategic shifts, and annual planning for major initiatives. Build in flexibility to respond to market changes and seasonal opportunities without derailing your overall strategy.

Ultimately, your budget is more than just numbers on a spreadsheet. It's the backbone of your GTM strategy, enabling you to move forward with confidence, clarity, and control. Whether you're entering the market for the first time or scaling up, your budget—aligned with the phases of the marketing cycle—ensures that your vision becomes a reality both efficiently and effectively. The last thing you want to do is fall for these common budgeting pitfalls:

- Spreading resources too thin across too many channels

- Abandoning initiatives before they've had sufficient time to show results

- Failing to account for creative development and production costs

- Neglecting to budget for optimization and iteration of campaigns

- Overlooking the true cost of customer acquisitions when planning growth targets

To get started, building a budgetary sheet that breaks down your objectives, priorities, and resources is crucial. This should include sections for foundational elements (Phase One), channel testing and experimentation (Phase Two), and scaling what works (Phase Three). By organizing your budget in this way, you'll have a clear, actionable roadmap that keeps you focused and adaptable as your business grows.

Below, I have built an example of a budgetary sheet that you can use to fill in details of your business's budget.

Marketing Budget Allocation Framework

Core Budget Allocation (75 – 80 percent of Total Budget)

Marketing Category	Startup (0 – 2 years)	Growth (2 – 5 years)	Established (5+ years)	Notes
Brand Awareness	25 – 30%	15 – 20%	10 – 15%	Building recognition vs. maintaining presence
Lead Generation	50 – 55%	60 – 65%	40 – 50%	Primary revenue driver, varies by sales cycle
Tools & Infrastructure	20 – 25%	5 – 10%	5 – 10%	Higher initial setup, then maintenance
Customer Retention	0 – 5%	15 – 20%	35 – 40%	Grows with customer base maturity
Subtotal	100%	100%	100%	

Figure 3.5: Core Budget Allocation Example

Additional Budget Components (20 – 25% of Total Budget)

Category	Allocation	Purpose	Timeline
Testing & Optimization	5 – 10%	Channel experimentation and A/B testing	Three- to six-month cycles
Scaling Reserve	5 – 10%	Double down on proven channels	Quarterly reallocation
Pivot Fund	5 – 10%	Quick shifts to better-performing channels	As needed
Subtotal	**15 – 30%**		

Figure 3.6: Additional Budget Components

Complete Budget Structure

Component	Percentage of Total	Purpose
Core Operations	75 – 80%	Day-to-day marketing activities
Growth & Testing	20 – 25%	Innovation and optimization
Total	**100%**	Complete marketing budget

Figure 3.7: Complete Budget Structure

Budget Performance Review Schedule

Maintaining a consistent review rhythm ensures timely course corrections and strategic optimization of your marketing investments. This structured approach (see chart above) to budget evaluation helps you to continuously identify both immediate opportunities and long-term trends that impact your marketing performance.

Now that we've established the business goals and measurable outcomes you want, we need to look outside the company's monetary gain. We need to look at loyalty, at gaining customers. How we do that is through creating a consistent, coherent, and compelling brand strategy framework.

Building Your Brand Strategy Framework

There's a lot we can do with the right framework for a company's objectives and budget, but in order to make a lasting, impactful brand that actually moves product, there are some key narrative components we need to build out. Remember in Chapter 1, we talked about how entrepreneurs valued story as a key element to their success, and in Chapter 2, we talked about the 4Ws. Well, this is where they all come together.

What you are building now is your brand strategy framework—your definitive guide to your business and its distinctive value in the market. The ideas that follow are your guiding principles, underpinning every endeavor you take and how you present yourself to the world. Throughout my career, a lot of founders will dismiss writing these values, ideas, and personalities out, knowing they have them in their mind. But actually conducting the exercise of it, putting pen to paper, solidifies everything. You can more clearly see what you are doing, why you are doing it, who you are doing it for, and the way you want to stand out and distinguish yourself in the market. This is an extremely important part of Phase One, without which you'll constantly be losing time, money, and energy, which can lead to burnout for your team and yourself. If you take the time to do these exercises and write out your ideas for each key framework component, you'll be ahead of the rest—and your audience will feel it too.

Quick Pitch

Your quick pitch is a succinct, yet powerful encapsulation of your business's unique value proposition. It serves as a compelling snapshot of what your business does, why it matters, and how it stands out. Think of your quick pitch as a tiered message designed to engage listeners on three levels—each corresponding to a specific timeframe. The reason why we do this is to get you down to being able to speak to your business in a clean and concise manner, whether you only have three seconds or an hour. Here's the 3-10-30 method that I use with my clients to develop their ideal quick pitch:

1. **3 Seconds:** This is your hook, a high-level description of your business that grabs attention immediately. It's often referred to as your "single most selling message." If you had just one sentence to describe your business, what would it be?

2. **10 Seconds:** If your listener is intrigued, this next level explains the *way* of your business, diving deeper into what makes your business unique.

3. **30 Seconds:** This is where you unfold the full narrative. It incorporates your *why*, *who*, *what*, and *way*, offering a more comprehensive understanding of your mission and the specific value you bring to your audience.

Each tier builds upon the last, creating a seamless flow that engages your audience step by step, ensuring you capture and maintain their interest. When you do this, you'll be able to really narrow down how you speak about your business. As Steve Jobs once said, "Simple can be harder than complex: You have to work hard to get your thinking clean to make it simple."

Breaking the quick pitch down into these tiers ensures that your pitch is flexible, adaptable, and laser-focused, whether you're meeting potential investors, engaging customers, or networking at events. Perfecting your quick pitch means you're prepared to capture attention and inspire action in any scenario.

When you focus on these tiers, you want to hit a component of each of your 4Ws. Depending on how much time you have, here's an outline for which W aligns with what tier:

- *What:* The focus of your 3-second hook.

- *Way:* Highlighted in the 10-second explanation of your process or methodology.

- *Why and Who:* Brought to life in the 30-second full narrative, connecting your mission to your audience.

Think of what goes into your quick pitch as the raw material that forms the foundation for all your marketing strategies and storytelling. It distills the essence of your business into a compact, memorable format. When you write your quick pitch, focus on clarity, brevity, and impact. While your quick pitch may not always make it to the market as a stand-alone message, it serves a greater purpose: helping you get crystal clear about how you talk about your business. When done right, your quick pitch forms the backbone of your brand's identity and helps transform casual interactions into meaningful opportunities. As you learn more about the phases, you'll be coming back to this often, as it will inspire the full-length feature of your marketing campaigns and storytelling.

Mission and Vision

Your mission is the essence of your business—the deeper dive into your *why* that informs every decision, from product development to marketing campaigns and customer service. Far from being a set of lofty ideals or filler text for your website, your mission is a guidepost that steers your business's day-to-day operations, anchoring its purpose in clarity and intention.

Meanwhile, your vision is your perpetual North Star, a vivid and compelling image of the future you're working toward. Rooted in the *why* and *way* of your 4Ws, it defines your aspirations and the unique approach you take to achieve them. Unlike a fixed milestone, your vision bridges the immediate focus of your mission with the long-term trajectory of your business, evolving as you reach goals and set new ones. Essentially, mission and vision are a pair that feed off each other, where mission is in the here and now and vision is the long-term.

Let's look at a B2B and B2C example to understand how mission and vision work together, but still have their own roles to play in building your brand strategy framework. Keep in mind, we will use the same company example throughout the whole exercise to keep it consistent.

In a *B2B* context of a software company, your mission might be: "To simplify complex business logistics through intuitive, scalable software solutions." This speaks to a purpose beyond just selling software—it highlights making businesses' lives easier, the why behind what you do, and it can be achieved here and now because this is why they built their business. However, in the same context, the B2B's vision statement might look like this: "To become the most trusted partner for businesses navigating operational complexity—empowering teams worldwide with software that feels seamless, smart, and built to grow with them." Here, the *why* (evolution) highlights innovation and transformation, while the *way* (remote work) emphasizes collaboration and accessibility, pushing the company to its long-term goal of helping create a more interconnected worldwide workforce.

In a *B2C* scenario, like a sustainable fashion brand focusing on fitness apparel, your mission could be: "To cut fashion's carbon footprint by making sustainable, ethically made fitness apparel the everyday choice." This tells you, your staff, and your audience that you don't want to sell just any clothes. It emphasizes the type of product you have as well as the values of quality and ethical production from day one. The same fashion brand's vision statement might be: "To redefine fashion as a force for good—where style, sustainability, and fairness come together, and every wardrobe choice creates a better world." This showcases the *why* (empowerment) and the *way* (through stylish, functional products) and highlights the trajectory of contributing to and creating a better world.

In both cases, the mission becomes a driver of strategy. The B2B software company will put its marketing efforts into initiatives that emulate and reflect the mission, like white papers or case studies, to show its efficiency gains to prospective clients. The sustainable fashion brand might rely on social media campaigns that show behind-the-scenes transparency, such as factory processes and sustainable sourcing, reinforcing their commitment to ethical production.

The mission also serves as a cultural cornerstone within your organization. Internally, it aligns employees with the broader purpose of their work, motivating them and providing a standard for decision-making. Externally, it positions your brand as intentional and purpose-driven, resonating with investors, partners, and customers alike.

Your vision serves as a guide and tool for the long term: Internally, it presents a unifying goal that aligns departments, teams, and strategies, giving them a sense of purpose and long-term investment of their career time to your company. Like customers, people want to work for a company that has a mission, so they feel fulfilled in their work too. A vision is a great way to give them that sense of fulfillment and clarity of what they are contributing to. Externally, your vision tells your target audience, investors, partners, and so on that you don't just plan to be a one-and-done company. You are aiming to be around for the long term because of your why, and you have ways in which you want to achieve it.

Importantly, achieving your vision isn't the end—it's a new beginning. Every milestone broadens your horizon, requiring you to refine and expand your vision to adapt to new realities and possibilities. By celebrating accomplishments and using them as stepping stones, your vision remains a dynamic force that not only inspires great achievements but also sets the stage for sustainable, impactful growth.

Whether launching a new product, entering a new market, or planning a major acquisition, having a clear mission and vision keeps each move aligned with your why. Next, you'll see how mission and vision become the *whys* that motivate every *what* and *how* in your decision-making process.

Unique Value Proposition

Your unique value proposition (UVP) is the heartbeat of your business—the *way* of your 4Ws that sets you apart from competitors. A well-crafted UVP distills the essence of what makes you unique, why your product or service matters, and how it solves a specific problem for your audience in a way no one else can, or it delivers solutions more efficiently, effectively, or enjoyably than others.

In a *B2B* context, your UVP might emphasize efficiency, cost savings, or innovative technology. The same software company from above could say, "We turn tangled logistics into smooth momentum. Our software doesn't just manage operations—it liberates them, giving fast-moving teams the clarity and control to scale fearlessly." This UVP communicates both the way and the why. The *way* is through intuitive, scalable logistics software that simplifies complex workflows—offering a convenience other companies might not have, making them unique. The *why* is deeper: It empowers teams to move faster, feel more in control, and focus on growth. It meets the functional need for streamlined operations and the emotional need to feel confident and capable in a fast-paced business environment.

In a *B2C* setting, your UVP may focus on lifestyle, convenience, or emotional resonance. The same eco-focused fashion brand might have a UVP that says, "Wear what matters. Our pieces are stitched with purpose—bold, beautiful, and built to last—so you can look sharp without compromising your values or your wallet." This UVP also delivers the way and the why. The *way* is stylish, ethically made clothing that's accessible, delivering everyday convenience and personal style. But the *why* speaks louder: Shoppers want to look good *and* do good. It meets the functional need for high-quality, affordable fashion and the emotional need to align purchases with personal values like sustainability, fairness, and self-expression. To make your UVP stand out from other offerings in a meaningful way and connect to your audience, precision matters. Use solid, verifiable claims that demonstrate your value—like specific metrics or customer success stories. Credibility builds trust, and trust secures loyalty.

A strong UVP also functions as a compass within your *brand strategy framework,* guiding everything from product development to marketing messaging. Whether used in internal briefs, external campaigns, or casual conversations, your UVP ensures your messaging reflects not just *what* you do, but *how* and *why* you do it differently, consistently—which is a critical factor in capturing attention and building lasting relationships.

Keep in mind, you'll always face competitors, whether direct or indirect. What sets you apart is how effectively your UVP connects with your audience by addressing the gap they feel and fulfilling their specific needs. If you've identified this differentiation, you've taken a significant step in ensuring your business resonates with the right people. Done right, this will be the thread that ties together your brand's identity, ensuring clarity, alignment, and impact at every touchpoint.

Brand Promises

Internally, your brand promise is a guiding principle for your team, shaping decisions from product development to customer service. It acts as a quality control check: if a feature, partnership, or marketing campaign doesn't align with the promise, that feature, partnership, or campaign needs to be revisited and refined. This ensures every action reflects the essence of your brand.

Externally, a clear and consistent brand promise builds trust and simplifies decision-making for consumers. With countless options available, a strong promise reassures customers that choosing you is a reliable, beneficial decision they won't regret. However, meeting this promise consistently is crucial. Aspirational promises that exceed operational capabilities can erode trust—a loss that's hard to rebuild.

The types of promises, and how we make them, change depending on your business model. In the B2B world, your brand promise might highlight reliability, performance, and return on investment. For instance, continuing on the same tech company, your brand promise may read something like this: "We promise to remove the friction from your operations—delivering software that simplifies, scales, and supports your team every step of the way." The brand promise highlights how the company delivers intuitive, scalable software that simplifies operations (the what), because teams need clarity, speed, and confidence to grow effectively in complex business environments (the why).

For B2C brands, the focus often shifts to lifestyle, emotional benefits, or satisfaction. The same fashion brand might say: "We promise clothing that feels as good on your conscience as it does on your skin—designed to last, priced to include, and made with care for people and planet." The brand promise reflects the company's commitment to offering ethically made, high-quality clothing at accessible prices (the what), because today's consumers want to look good while staying true to their values and making responsible choices (the why).

For long-term impact, think of your brand promise as a cornerstone of your company's DNA. It doesn't just influence strategy and behavior. It forges deep connections with customers that go beyond transactions. By aligning with your why and addressing your who, your brand promise becomes the essence of what makes you, you. It's a statement of intent that influences internal culture, drives external perception, and creates a bond of trust that ensures your brand's longevity.

Boiler Plate Statement

A boilerplate statement is your company's public-facing identity, encapsulated in a concise, standardized paragraph. It serves as a go-to snapshot of your business, incorporating all the elements of your 4Ws:

- Who you are

- What you do

- Why it matters

- The way you uniquely operate

This is the business equivalent of your quick pitch in written form, designed for use at the end of press releases, in the "About Us" section of your website, or across various social media platforms. It offers a quick yet comprehensive understanding of your brand for journalists, prospective clients, and partners alike.

In the B2B world, boilerplate statements often highlight expertise, years of operation, and unique selling points, tailored to resonate with other businesses. For example: "[Company Name] is a business operations software company that helps teams simplify logistics and scale with confidence. Through intuitive, user-friendly platforms built for growth, the company removes complexity from day-to-day processes so businesses can focus on what matters most. Trusted by fast-moving teams across industries, [Company Name] transforms operational friction into momentum." This touches on *who* the company is, *what* it does, and its *way* of delivering value.

For B2C brands, boilerplates emphasize consumer needs and experiences. For instance: "[Brand Name] is a sustainable fashion label creating high-quality, ethically made clothing that's both stylish and accessible. With a focus on timeless design, responsible sourcing, and fair pricing, the brand makes it easy for customers to align their wardrobe with their values — without compromising on comfort or self-expression." This reflects the brand's *why* (ethical focus), *who* (style-conscious and socially aware consumers), and *way* (commitment to sustainability and quality).

A well-crafted boilerplate is more than just filler text. Internally, it serves as a benchmark for consistency in company-wide communications, ensuring that every team member presents a unified brand narrative. Externally, it acts as a pre-vetted descriptor that simplifies interactions with journalists, partners, and stakeholders, offering them a succinct yet accurate portrayal of your business. Regularly reviewing and updating it ensures alignment with changes in your strategy, branding, or target markets. This keeps your boilerplate adaptable and relevant. Ultimately, it is the condensed expression of your 4Ws, serving as a critical tool for clarity, consistency, and brand integrity. It allows anyone interacting with your company—whether internally or externally—to quickly grasp your core identity, ensuring that your message resonates across all platforms and scenarios.

As we transition from the external-facing elements that define how your business engages with the world, let's delve into the internal foundations—the cultural and operational frameworks that shape not only your company's core but also the way your brand is perceived externally. Believe it or not, what happens within your organization inevitably ripples outward, influencing how the world sees and interacts with your brand.

Charter

A company charter is not just a procedural document—it's the philosophical foundation of your business. It's a written testament to the ethos, ethics, and cultural norms that shape how you operate. More than outlining what your business does, your charter delves deeper into the why than the brand promise and boilerplate do, adding depth and texture to your corporate identity. It defines the principles that guide your objectives and the ways you achieve them.

In a B2B context, a charter might include

- **Supplier Relationships:** Establishing ethical and transparent dealings.

- **Client Engagement:** Maintaining trust, reliability, and mutual growth.

- **Innovation Standards:** Committing to cutting-edge, sustainable practices.

For B2C businesses, the charter could focus on

- **Customer Interaction Policies:** Prioritizing transparency, accessibility, and service excellence.

- **Community Involvement:** Outlining initiatives to give back and foster societal impact.

- **Sustainability Practices:** Committing to eco-friendly operations and product lifecycles.

The charter acts as an internal compass, guiding everyone from executives to interns. For new hires, it's a primer on your company's cultural DNA, ensuring alignment from day one. For seasoned employees, it serves as a reference for handling ethical dilemmas or strategic crossroads.

A charter's value grows as your business scales or pivots. Regular reviews and updates ensure it remains relevant, reflecting new challenges, opportunities, and market realities. However, evolving your charter doesn't mean abandoning your core identity. The best companies know how to stay relevant without losing themselves. Think of your charter like a tree: the roots (your core values and mission) stay planted deep, while the branches (your strategies and tactics) can grow and bend with changing conditions. When updating your charter, always ask: "Does this change support our fundamental why, or does it conflict with it?" Your original mission should remain the North Star, even as you adapt how you deliver on that purpose.

For example, if you started as a company focused on "making healthy living accessible," that core remains constant whether you're selling supplements, launching a fitness app, or expanding into meal planning services. The how evolves, but the why stays anchored. A static charter risks obsolescence, while an evolving one becomes a dynamic tool that helps your organization stay aligned, resilient, and future-focused, authentic to its roots.

Operational Personality

Operational personality goes beyond buzzwords—it's the unique DNA of your organization's day-to-day identity. It embodies the tone, style, and behavioral traits that shape how your business operates, internally and externally. While your *mission* defines *why* you exist and your *vision* outlines *where* you're headed, *operational personality* establishes *how* you'll achieve those goals. This applies to anything as overarching as leadership dynamics to as routine as daily customer interactions.

In B2B settings, operational personality might dictate the approach to client relationships:

- Are you highly consultative, tailoring solutions for each client's unique needs?

- Or do you focus on delivering standardized, high-quality products at scale?

For instance, a B2B consultancy may be more like the first option, prioritizing deep partnerships and customized solutions. This means the operational personality a B2B brand crafts should be collaborative, research-driven, and relationship-focused. In B2C, your operational personality often reflects the consumer experience, whether it's online, in-store, or both:

- A luxury brand may emphasize exclusivity and personal attention through VIP experiences.

- A fast-food chain might pride itself on speed, efficiency, and delivering value without compromising quality.

But operational personality isn't limited to external interactions—it's equally vital internally. How do your teams collaborate? Is decision-making hierarchical or egalitarian? Do you prioritize swift execution or deliberate planning? These characteristics inform everything from recruitment to training, ensuring alignment with your brand ethos.

As your business evolves, so should your operational personality. Revisit it during pivotal moments—mergers, expansions, or market shifts—to ensure it remains relevant and reflective of your organization's trajectory. This evolving identity not only reinforces who you are today but also serves as a roadmap for future growth.

Foundational Pillars

Your foundational pillars are the immutable principles and values that anchor your organization. They represent your *why*, *who*, and *way*—the elements that define your ethos and guide every decision, strategy, and interaction.

In B2B environments, these pillars often emphasize critical business principles:

- **Integrity:** Building trust through transparency and ethical practices.

- **Innovation:** Driving progress with cutting-edge solutions.

- **Customer Partnership:** Fostering long-term, collaborative relationships.

For example, a B2B software's pillars may look something like this:

- **Integrity**

  We build trust by operating with full transparency, ethical practices, and a commitment to doing what's right for our clients and their teams.

- **Innovation**

  We push boundaries by creating forward-thinking, scalable software that evolves with the needs of modern businesses.

- **Customer Partnership**

  We're more than a vendor—we're a long-term ally, working side-by-side with customers to solve problems and accelerate growth.

In B2C, these foundational elements often align with consumer expectations and experiences:

- **Quality:** Never sacrificing excellence for cost savings.
- **Affordability:** Providing value while maintaining high standards.
- **Community:** Giving back through initiatives that create social impact.

The sustainable fashion brand might structure its pillars with:

- **Quality**

  We craft every piece to last—choosing materials and construction that meet high standards without compromise.

- **Affordability**

  We believe conscious fashion should be accessible, delivering fair pricing without sacrificing style or ethics.

- **Community**

  We give back through socially impactful initiatives, empowering customers to support change every time they get dressed.

Internally, foundational pillars shape culture and performance. They can inform hiring practices, ensuring candidates align with your values. They can also serve as benchmarks for employee training, evaluations, and KPIs. Externally, they underpin marketing, partnerships, and brand positioning, making it easy to have a consistent and authentic narrative across all channels.

As the marketplace evolves, your pillars should remain steadfast but adaptable. Revisit them periodically so they continue to reflect your company's essence while aligning with new opportunities and challenges. These pillars are more than a guide—they're your organization's foundation, supporting everything you build today and tomorrow.

Target Customer Profile: Defining Your Brand's Core Audience

Once you've established your business foundations—marketing budget, company objectives, and brand strategy framework—it's time to get deeper into your customers' minds and walk a mile in their shoes.

Understanding Your Target Customer

When you started your business, you likely identified a market gap and had a specific customer in mind for your product or service. This aligns with the *who* in our 4W framework. However, as your business and offerings evolve, it's crucial to regularly review and adjust your messaging across all platforms, making sure you're still communicating effectively with your target audience(s). Effective communication means clearly addressing their pain points and demonstrating how you provide solutions. This applies whether you're just beginning your marketing journey or refining an existing customer profile.

A deeper understanding of your audience provides valuable insights into their language preferences and helps identify the most effective marketing platforms to reach them. Remember: what sets marketing apart across industries and companies is understanding who your specific audience is and where to find them.

Marketing Storytelling

When connecting with your audience, consider marketing storytelling as akin to a movie script. This isn't just about narrative—it's about creating an immersive experience that forges emotional connections between you and your audience, and guides your audience toward specific actions. By applying scriptwriting principles, marketers can develop more compelling and effective campaigns.

I want to tell you about the evolution of how we got to a place where marketing storytelling is the norm, not the exception. Hopefully, this will make things easier for you to build upon for your own company. I wish I could call this genius idea my own. I'm simplifying it for the purposes of this book, as it's actually a culmination of years of work in the making. (I am pivoting to storytelling with you, so bear with me!)

Marketing has always been rooted in storytelling—from the early days of radio soap operas sponsored by Procter & Gamble in the 1930s to today's sophisticated brand narratives. This evolution wasn't sparked by a single individual but developed gradually through many contributors. Academic scholars like Barbara Stern began analyzing advertisements as literary texts in the 1990s, while around the same time, business thinkers like Rolf Jensen predicted a shift to an "imagination economy," where companies would sell dreams rather than just products.

By the early 2000s, marketers were openly discussing campaigns in terms of plots and character arcs. Books like *Hero and the Outlaw* by Margaret Mark encouraged brands to position themselves as archetypal characters within larger narratives, while influential voices like Seth Godin popularized the idea with statements like, "Marketing is no longer about the stuff that you make, but about the stories you tell." Marketing campaigns themselves began to resemble Hollywood productions.

While Donald Miller wasn't the first to connect marketing and storytelling, his StoryBrand framework (introduced around 2015 – 2017) was revolutionary in making the concept practical and accessible. Modeled after movie scripts and inspired by Joseph Campbell's Hero's Journey—outlined in *The Hero with a Thousand Faces*—Miller's method positions the customer as the hero, the brand as the guide, and the marketing message as a clear path to resolution. He turned timeless storytelling principles into a step-by-step screenplay-style template for businesses to create effective marketing campaigns. In today's marketing landscape (2026), storytelling has evolved even further. Brands now leverage AI to personalize narratives at scale, creating individualized "hero journeys" for different customer segments. Interactive experiences like augmented reality, virtual spaces, and creator collaborations have turned audiences from passive listeners into active participants in brand stories. Meanwhile, authenticity has become the new currency: Customers respond more to imperfect, relatable storytelling than to polished perfection. As technology advances and consumer expectations shift, storytelling remains at the heart of marketing—but it is now more personalized, participatory, and human than ever before.

The most successful companies today don't just sell products. They invite consumers to play roles in ongoing brand narratives. This approach works because humans are naturally wired to respond to stories more deeply than to facts or features alone. The marketing plan is no longer just a strategy document—it's the blueprint for a story waiting to be told.

So how can you apply this to your own marketing? Here, let's take the elements that make up a great, compelling story for books and movies and turn them into marketing blocks that tell the story to consumers.

- **Characters: Your Brand's Hero Journey**. Think of your brand as the mentor and your customer as the hero. Like a film protagonist, your customer faces challenges, while your brand—like a wise guide—provides the tools and support they need to overcome obstacles. Your products and services become the magical tools in their journey of transformation.

- **Plot: Mapping the Customer's Story.** Just as movies follow a narrative arc, your customer's journey unfolds in stages: They begin facing a challenge (exposition), search for answers (rising action), discover your solution (climax), implement it (falling action), and finally experience transformation (resolution). This journey showcases their evolution from their initial state to their empowered position after engaging with your brand.

- **Conflict: Addressing Pain Points**. Every compelling story needs tension. In marketing, your customers' pain points create this narrative tension. By acknowledging these challenges and demonstrating how your offerings resolve them, you create a powerful resolution that resonates with your audience.

- **Theme: Your Brand's Core Message.** Like a film's central message, your brand values form the foundation of your story. When these values align with your audience's beliefs and aspirations, they create lasting connections that go beyond simple transactions.

- **Emotion: Creating Meaningful Connections and Understanding Their Needs**. Films move us because they tap into universal emotions. Similarly, effective marketing creates emotional resonance by helping customers feel understood, valued, and empowered. Your brand story should evoke specific feelings that align with your customers' desires and aspirations.

- **Narrative Tools: Crafting Your Story.** Just as filmmakers use various techniques to enhance their storytelling, marketers employ tools like social proof, testimonials, and visual storytelling to strengthen their message and deepen audience engagement.

The fundamentals of storytelling remain consistent across all industries, built on characters, plot, conflict, theme, emotion, and narrative devices, whether in traditional advertisements or social media clips. These elements create a framework that captivates audiences and drives action, regardless of what you're marketing. However, your story's effectiveness ultimately depends on your audience. Success lies in understanding who they are, what challenges they face, what motivates them, and where to reach them.

The real impact comes from both crafting a compelling narrative and carefully tailoring it to resonate with your specific audience, presenting it where they're most likely to engage—whether through social media, content marketing, email campaigns, or in-person interactions. Maintaining consistent messaging across all channels is crucial. Any inconsistency risks confusing your customers.

Ideal Customer Profile

Your ideal customer profile (ICP) is a detailed representation of the customers most likely to benefit from—and engage with—your product or service. It connects what you do, how you do it, and why you do it to the people you're doing it for. This foundational element drives smart marketing strategies and strong business decisions.

Many businesses have multiple ICPs based on their product lines or services. But even within a single ICP, there are often tiers or segments—individuals who are ready to convert, those who are exploring options, and others who need more education before taking action. These aren't different customers—they're the same ideal profile at different stages of the buyer journey.

Understanding and addressing this layered reality allows you to tailor your messaging more effectively.

A truly effective ICP goes far beyond surface-level demographics. It should include

- **Demographics and firmographics (for B2B):** Age, location, industry, company size, and revenue

- **Psychographics and behavior patterns:** Values, motivations, online habits, and content preferences

- **Goals and readiness signals:** What drives their decisions and what outcomes they seek

- **Decision-making roles:** Who influences the purchase, who approves it, and who uses it

One important distinction to make is that the end user isn't always the decision-maker. For example, more of a B2C example, a toy may be designed for a child, but the person making the decision to purchase it is the parent. Your marketing must speak to both audiences: the emotional connection for the end user, and the rational or values-based messaging for the buyer. This may mean creating different content or website pages targeted to each role in the buying process.

Understanding your ideal customer at this depth provides you with the following benefits: You can now

- Tailor messaging that truly resonates

- Focus marketing efforts on the most promising channels

- Guide product development to meet specific needs

- Maximize marketing ROI

- Build long-term customer loyalty

- Develop brand ambassadors organically

- Align sales and marketing teams around a shared target

- Improve customer onboarding and retention strategies

Here's where the customer journey, as described in Chapter 2, comes into play. A clear path can guide customers from pain to progress by identifying their needs and wants, showing your expertise by offering tailored solutions. After assessing the customer journey, you can now develop content that matches what they believe will make them the hero, and you are helping them with their decision-making process to make their dream a reality. Remember: Brands that successfully make the customer the hero don't just tell stories—they build journeys where the customer sees themselves as the protagonist moving toward a better future. The most effective brands follow steps like these:

1. **Know Your Hero**: Identify your audience's key characteristics, needs, and aspirations. For example, Nike didn't sell shoes—it sold the idea that *you* are an athlete, no matter your level. Their campaigns tap directly into the consumer's identity and aspirations—to be an athlete or at least feel like one!

2. **Understand Their Challenge**: Pinpoint the specific problems or obstacles your audience faces. Make these pain points concrete and relatable. Dove's *Real Beauty* campaign identified a deep emotional challenge—how women perceive their own beauty—and addressed that pain point head-on, making it personal and relatable.

3. **Present Your Solution**: Position your company as the comprehensive answer to their challenges, offering a complete toolkit of products and services that directly address their

needs. GoPro positioned its cameras as the tool that enables everyday adventurers to capture and share their heroic moments. The product became the enabler, not the focus.

4. **Educate your Hero, Establish Your Authority, and Tell your Story**: Demonstrate your expertise and capability to solve their problems. Show why your solution is uniquely qualified to address their specific challenges. Apple masterfully combines authority with storytelling—showing how its ecosystem makes life simpler, more creative, and more powerful. Their ads and retail experiences continually educate while reinforcing the brand's role as a trusted guide.

5. **Paint the Before and After**: Create a vivid contrast between two futures: one where they've implemented your solution and are thriving, and another where they've maintained the status quo and continue to face challenges. Make the transformation concrete and compelling. Consider Peloton. Its messaging paints a vivid picture: before, you're stuck in uninspired workouts; after, you're part of a motivated, connected community achieving your fitness goals.

6. **Guide Their Next Steps**: Instead of just saying "call to action," use "action path" or "next steps," present a clear, simple pathway for engagement that feels natural and achievable. Break down exactly what getting started looks like and emphasize its simplicity. Successful brands like Amazon remove friction at the critical decision moment. From one-click purchasing to tailored recommendations, they present an effortless path forward that feels natural and empowering. Similarly, Sephora creates this experience in person at checkout by offering sample-sized products for purchase, encouraging additional purchases during future visits.

Unfortunately, most conversions online are lost at the add to cart. There is a big drop for most brands, so solving this means optimizing your website, funnel, and so on is key. This is another crucial area for testing and learning as you become more established and move on to the different marketing phases.

The Three Audiences

Let's talk about something that often gets overlooked—you actually have more than just one target audience. I know, I know. Most people think they should focus on just one ideal customer, but successful businesses usually need to connect with at least three different groups. Why three, you ask? Let's think about it this way:

First, you've got the people who actually use your product or service. These are your primary users. They're the ones who experience it firsthand and know exactly how it makes their life better. But here's the catch—they might not be the ones with the power to buy it.

That brings us to your second audience: the decision-makers. These folks hold the purse strings. Maybe it's the CEO, the procurement team, or even parents buying for their kids. While they might never actually use your product themselves, they need to be convinced it's worth investing in.

Then there's your third audience—the influencers or recommenders. These are the people others turn to for advice. In business settings, these could be industry experts, consultants, or trusted advisors. In consumer markets, think friends, family members, online reviewers, or social media influencers. Whether it's a procurement consultant recommending software to a CEO or a friend recommending a restaurant to their social circle, these influencers need to feel confident that recommending you won't damage their reputation or relationships.

Each of these audiences requires different messaging approaches:

- Primary users need to understand how your solution makes their lives easier.

- Decision-makers need to see clear value and return on their investment.

- Influencers need compelling reasons to recommend you while protecting their reputation.

But don't worry—just because you have three different target audiences doesn't mean you need three completely different marketing approaches. It's more about tweaking your message while keeping your core story consistent. Think of it like telling the same story but highlighting different parts depending on who's listening, as each one is going to have a different pain point of focus.

Let's revert to the project management software example for a moment. When talking to the actual users (project managers), you'd want to highlight how it saves them two hours of admin work daily and reduces the stress of juggling multiple deadlines. This is huge for the primary users and makes their day-to-day easier. However, when presenting to the CEO, you lead with how it increases team productivity by 30 percent and reduces project delays that cost the company money. These are the people who have the purchasing power to get the project managers what they need, but they need to see a benefit to themselves, too. Otherwise, the product doesn't hold much value. And when the CEO is speaking to the IT consultant they trust, you emphasize to the IT team the seamless integration capabilities and robust security features that protect their reputation when they recommend solutions. Same product, same core benefits—but you're speaking directly to what keeps each target audience up at night. The project manager cares about their daily workload, the CEO cares about the bottom line, and the consultant cares about recommending something that won't blow up in their face. Hit the right pain point, and suddenly everyone's listening.

The magic happens when you get all three groups nodding along with your message. That's when you've got a marketing strategy that really works—because you're speaking to everyone who has a say in your success, not just one group.

Remember, these groups often talk to each other too. Your users might influence the decision-makers, who might check in with industry experts. When you understand these connections, you can create marketing that flows naturally between all three groups.

Phase One Wrap-Up: Foundation Complete, What's Coming Next?

Understanding your audiences, crafting your story, building your marketing budget, and setting company objectives are just the foundations. Now comes the exciting part: putting it all into action. You've got your foundation set, you know who you're talking to, and you've got your story straight. But how do you actually make it all work? How do you turn these ideas into real, measurable results? That's exactly what we're diving into next. Welcome to Phase Two: *Propel*, where we turn your vision into action.

CHAPTER 4

PHASE TWO: PROPEL

Compose Your Symphony of Strategy

Set your target and keep trying until you reach it.
– Napoleon Hill

Now that we have Phase One: Prepare all set, let's roll up our sleeves and plunge into Phase Two: Propel. This is where strategy takes center stage, and you launch your marketing out into the world. With your foundation set, we will now focus on creating the systems and strategy you need to reach your market: your online presence, establishing your data metrics to track achievements, assigning clear responsibilities, and building your GTM strategy for a successful market debut.

Here you will develop your marketing plan, hit launch, then begin testing and learning. Phase Two moves you through planning and into action, putting your strategy to work and gathering the insights that will drive your future optimization efforts. You can't expect to meet, let alone exceed, your quarterly and yearly targets without a road map. And you definitely can't recognize growth if you don't define what it looks like beforehand. This phase, done right, should function like a well-oiled machine moving toward a shared vision.

Once you've built your website or social media effectively to communicate your brand's narrative that we built in Phase One, we will get your *martech* stack—your marketing technology tools—connected to link every detail and aspect, ultimately allowing you to track a signup from your website all the way to a sale and everything in between. These tools should be more than just a collection of software; they need to form an interconnected ecosystem ready to capture, analyze, and interpret data from every touchpoint. You don't need many to be effective.

We will then build your GTM strategy that becomes your battle plan, your playbook, your secret sauce. It enables rapid A/B testing—a method of comparing two versions of any content marketing asset to determine which performs better—across multiple variations of your messaging, landing pages, content, and creative outlets to understand what resonates with your audience and what doesn't.

Marketing Tools Stack: Your Company's Website/Social Channel

Your website is the principal introduction to your business, presenting the key aspects: Who you are, what you do, why you exist, and the way you do what you do that sets you apart from your competitors. Alongside this, social media accounts play a significant role as well, though the importance of this varies depending on the nature of your industry. Many businesses, in fact, establish their social media presence even before they develop a website due to the ease of setup. Social platforms can manage bookings, sales, advertisements—the whole gamut. On the flipside, some businesses may never need a social platform to thrive, but it could be an added bonus.

For entrepreneurs just starting out, even a simple one-page website can be crucial. A website serves as your digital business card, anchoring your online presence, while your social channels drive engagement. This one-pager should, at minimum, clearly communicate your value proposition and provide contact information, establishing credibility beyond what social platforms alone can offer.

When appropriate, integrating your personal brand with your business presence can significantly strengthen customer connections. No matter the industry, building a personal brand has definitely helped many businesses with conversions, as it creates trust, and when people trust you, it makes it easier to sell. Today's consumers often want to know the people behind the products or services they purchase. Your authentic personal story, expertise, and values can become powerful differentiators that not only connect with audiences emotionally but are increasingly favored by social algorithms. While it's a common misconception that visibility online requires chasing trends or compromising authenticity, platforms like LinkedIn, Instagram, and even Google increasingly prioritize content that sparks genuine engagement—posts that receive meaningful comments, shares, and saves, rather than just fleeting likes.

A lot of conversations around AI and how it can replace authenticity have surfaced. I think authenticity will never be replaced by AI, and consumers will begin to look more for the real people and products—the ones they can believe in and trust. Audiences today are drawn to real stories and values they can relate to, and algorithms reward that sustained, genuine interaction.

This is especially important for consultants, service providers, and businesses where *you* are the face of the brand. By leaning into what makes you unique and behaving authentically, you not only stand out but also build long-term credibility and loyalty—all without having to game the system or dilute your message.

Your personal brand can extend far beyond your website and social media channels—it might include speaking at industry events, hosting webinars, appearing on podcasts (or hosting your own), publishing articles, participating in community initiatives, or even growing your influencer presence. Each of these touchpoints creates additional opportunities to connect with potential customers in meaningful ways while building your authority in your field and presenting your authentic self. Consider how influential figures in your industry have leveraged their personal brand to elevate their business: They likely maintain a consistent presence across multiple platforms, share thought-leadership content, and create memorable experiences that keep their audience engaged. This omnichannel approach to personal branding creates multiple entry points for customers to discover your business, often through connecting with you as an individual first. For service-based businesses especially, clients often choose to work with you because of who you are and your specific approach, making your personal brand inseparable from your business success.

While this approach may yield amazing results, it might not be the most beneficial for some businesses. But the key is this:

Both websites and social platforms could be truly supportive of one another. Ideally, your social channels should serve as engagement hubs that funnel interested prospects to your website, where conversion happens. As you will always see and hear me mention, the importance of engagement to conversion—really everything we do in marketing—lies in the interconnectedness of various elements that make your business thrive both online and offline.

Among these interconnected elements, your website serves as a critical cornerstone for your local and organic SEO efforts, which involve optimizing a website to naturally rank higher in search engine results without paid advertising. Don't beat a dead horse with semantics in building out your brand architecture content. The copy will need to resonate with what prospects are searching for, and sometimes, you can do that better in fewer words than more. Even a concise website, comprised of just one, two, or three well-crafted pages, can help your business rank higher on Google and be discovered by potential customers. In addition, most businesses forget or delay this part, but tools like Google My Business act as an extension of your website—boosting SEO, supporting surveys and reviews, and helping customers find and trust your business more easily. It also provides insights into search terms, clicks, calls, and direction requests—along with customer listening through reviews and feedback—to refine your marketing. Therefore, having a website is a fundamental step in your digital strategy. Having a higher SEO can bring people back to your social channel.

The ebb and flow of traffic between your website and social media are truly reliant on one another. Engagement on socials leads to interest and conversions on your website, and your website's strong SEO will take people to your socials, where they can engage with you and your products, further enhancing your story and prospects. Both are avenues where your target audience gets to know who you are and why you do what you do.

Building your website is both an art and a science, requiring careful thought on how you'd like visitors to navigate your content and take the actions you have put forth. A proven approach is to pay close attention to UI/UX (User Interface and User Experience). UI is a concept that refers to the design, layout, and organization of your site's interactive elements; UX is the overall experience a user has while interacting with your website and navigating through the various pages, ultimately ending in a main call to action that you establish, getting the prospect to move into your top funnel where potential customers are first introduced to a brand or product. These both focus on awareness, consideration, and engagement, and are a crucial aspect that directly impacts a customer's journey and their interaction with your website.

You can learn a lot about how UX/UI affects your customers' experience by looking at your competitors and indirect competitors—and you can do this before you even go to market! One thing you can learn is SEO, as mentioned in the next steps. But the major, most crucial reason is understanding if your website adheres to best practices.

Here is where looking at indirect and direct competitors in your industry to see how they are navigating their UI/UX is a must. You should definitely look at the "best in class" competitors within the industry to really understand UI/UX as a whole. Auditing what they are doing in comparison to you (not to compare, but if they have been in business for a while and are successful, they must be doing something right) gives you the perspective to see what works for your target audience, what doesn't, what applies to your brand and how you want to do things so you can build your best website before launching. On the flip side, looking at indirect competitors or sites that are doing things well can help you identify opportunities to stand out in your own industry by doing what others aren't. There is a best practice set up out there, and I have built a template that will support your brand narrative and navigable UI/UX design—meaning more consumers taking action based on your guidance. This is where I want to emphasize A/B testing your home page and multiple other pages, so you can really get your website to be one of the higher-performing pages on the internet. Lastly: Choose a website platform with built-in accessibility features—such as templates that support screen readers, captions, and inclusive design—so your site is usable by people who are deaf, blind, or have other disabilities.

Take a look at my very simplistic template of a website. This is a suggested homepage blueprint to either build out your initial business or to optimize your current layout. Test it, learn from it. Starting from here, this is a blank canvas. As you see how your audience navigates it, change and adjust it, getting to the ideal layout that optimizes your target audience's experience with your personal brand. Keep in mind the homepage is your website's most important page because it's usually the first thing visitors see, and you only have seconds to make a good impression before they decide to stay or leave. It serves as the main hub that guides people to everything else on your site while establishing your credibility and clearly communicating what you do and why they should care. Since most of your website traffic flows through the homepage, it's often the make-or-break point for converting visitors into customers. You may, down the road, create dedicated pages that serve as landing spots to drive marketing traffic into an action, which is part of your marketing funnel. Still, your homepage remains the foundation that everything else builds upon.

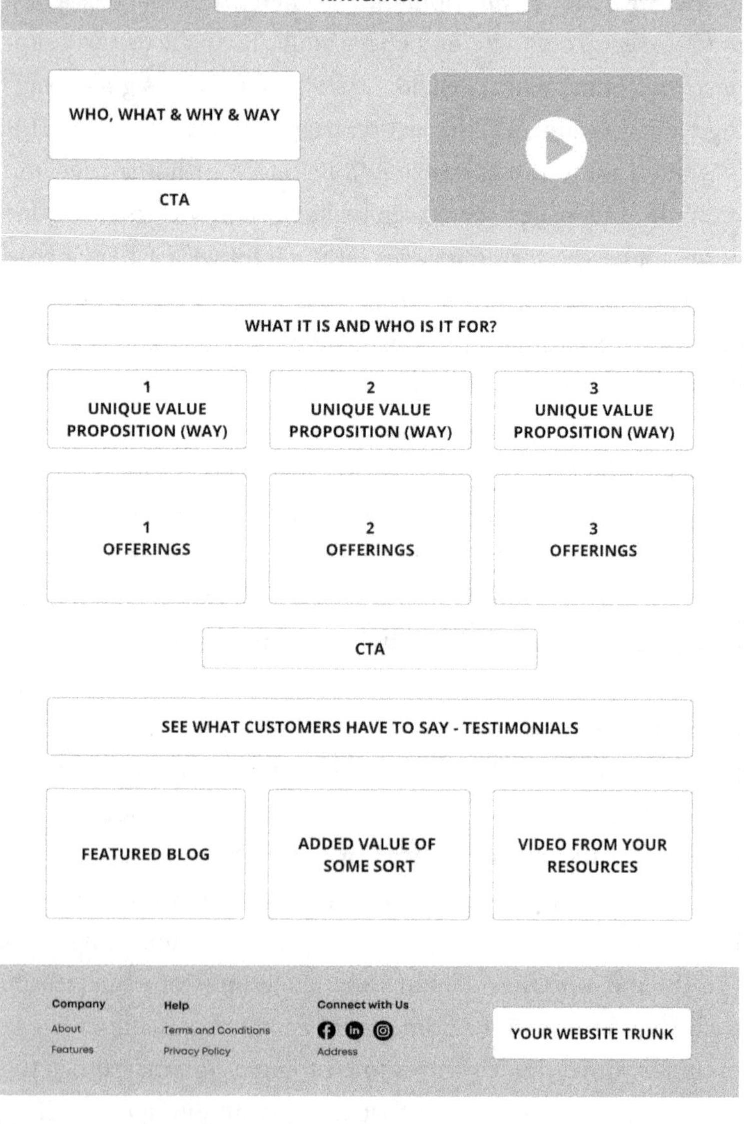

Figure 4.1: Template Website Layout

Much of the content you develop for your website will and should likely be drawn from your brand strategy framework document, hence this being one of the first steps in getting your message for content in a good place. When working with the expertise of a marketer, this content can be optimized with carefully selected keywords that can bolster your organic SEO and local SEO growth. You can start to see now how all the components interconnect. Of course, drawing from your competitors, both indirect and direct, to understand how they are doing their marketing is also crucial, as your goal is to potentially outpace them within the organic SEO space and ensure your website is in best-practice mode across the board.

To round this up, SEO is particularly important as it is one of marketing's foundational and most cost-effective strategies that, when implemented correctly from the onset, continues to yield benefits for your business over time. As I like to say, it is the "gift that keeps on giving." Therefore, it's paramount not to delay optimizing your website for organic SEO. It's like a fine wine; SEO gets better over time, because it takes time for the engine to rev up and for Google to recognize, rank, and index your business, especially if you are brand new.

Whether you begin with a robust website or start with just social channels and a simple one-pager, what matters most is establishing a consistent online presence that authentically represents both your personal and business brand. As your business grows, your digital presence can evolve alongside it—expanding your website functionality and optimizing the connection between your social channels and website conversion paths. To postpone this process could be detrimental (not life or death to your business, but more like a crying shame and a missed opportunity on filling your top funnel and revenue steam type of way), especially considering that SEO could potentially emerge as your most effective marketing channel, or it may only ever be what you do in marketing to gain net new prospects through your funnel.

Marketing Tools Stack: Tracking Your Efforts

We've briefly touched on your *martech* stack, but let's dig in a little deeper. A marketing tool stack is the collection of technologies that your company uses to execute and analyze marketing activities. This stack typically involves software systems for various purposes, ranging from content creation and project management to CRM. These systems manage interactions with current and potential customers, streamline processes, and improve profitability by managing email marketing, data analytics, customer support, and automating tasks that can be removed from your daily workload. AI has always excelled at this, and it is only getting better with time.

Having the right few tools (note: *few* tools, as we talked about previously) in place will ensure your company gets the insights it needs. Believe me, more is not better. Don't sign up for whatever you are marketed to do. Here, the idea is that less is more, and understanding what platforms can support multiple efforts is key. I always say the fewer logins one has to do on a daily basis, the simpler the daily tasks stay, so the best thing is to figure out where you can consolidate and what platforms offer more than just one lane of support.

A tech startup I worked with had over forty tools on their list—half of which they were paying for but not even using. This is more common than you'd think. When starting out, it's easy to sign up for a bunch of tools and then forget about them if you're not keeping a close eye. Don't let that money go to waste—those funds could be better spent on things like marketing. So many businesses leave money on the table. Don't be one of them.

Here are the five key reasons why an effective, curated marketing tech tool stack is important:

Increased Efficiency with Automation

Investing in a well-integrated marketing tool stack is akin to hiring a virtual team of specialists, dedicated to automating repetitive tasks. Some larger companies take this concept and build it on their own, but why build it when there are perfected systems in place? This isn't just about cutting down the time to post updates on social media or send out emails. It's about freeing up your creative and strategic minds from menial tasks so they can focus on what they do best—planning, storytelling, and analyzing data—essentially, building the business. Artificial intelligence is accelerating this automation at breakneck speeds. For startups and small to mid-sized businesses, this means being able to do more with less, making it increasingly viable to compete with larger enterprises in terms of marketing sophistication.

In a B2B setting, the efficiency gains could be monumental. When mundane tasks are automated, your team can focus on deepening relationships with key accounts. Consider a robust CRM system that automatically segments your clients and leads. This lets you tailor content and communication to each segment, something that would otherwise be a manual and time-consuming effort.

For B2C businesses, the automation capabilities of a marketing tool stack enable personalized customer engagement at an unprecedented scale. Imagine a scenario where a tool segments customers by their buying history, location, and engagement with past campaigns. You have targeted, specific data, so no longer are you forced to blanket-blast a generic newsletter. Now, you're reaching out with personalized product recommendations or location-specific offers, potentially increasing your conversion rates substantially.

Be mindful that although automation is fabulous, it's not a set-it-and-forget-it deal. These tools require ongoing oversight. Startups need to constantly review performance metrics and adjust strategies to ensure these automated activities are delivering the desired ROI. The efficiency of your marketing stack is not just about the capabilities of individual tools. It's also about how seamlessly they integrate with each other. For instance, data from your social media campaigns should flow effortlessly into your analytics tool, which should then integrate flawlessly into your CRM. This unbroken data chain allows for more cohesive and informed decision-making. Automation offers incremental improvements, which can be a game-changer for startups and small businesses. It opens the door for transformative changes in how you approach marketing, enabling you to act like a much larger operation without the need for a massive team or budget. By streamlining repetitive tasks, enhancing personalization, and allowing for real-time insights and adjustments, a well-designed marketing stack empowers your business to compete in both B2B and B2C spaces more effectively than ever before.

Beyond basic automation, today's AI-powered marketing tools are revolutionizing how businesses operate. Sophisticated machine learning algorithms can now predict customer behaviors, automatically optimize ad spending, generate compelling content, and personalize experiences at scale. Imagine tools that can write email subject lines with higher open rates than human marketers from years of cumulative research, or algorithms that automatically adjust your bidding strategy across advertising platforms to maximize ROI. These aren't futuristic concepts—they're available now and becoming increasingly accessible to businesses of all sizes. The businesses that embrace these AI capabilities for marketing optimization gain not just incremental efficiency but potentially transformative advantages over competitors still relying on traditional methods.

Data Insights and Decision-Making

Think of data as the raw fuel powering your startup's marketing engine. Advanced analytics tools are your refineries, converting this oil into actionable insights. These are not just nifty gadgets but essential components in understanding customer behaviors, gauging campaign performance, and spotting emerging trends in the market.

In a B2B context, analytics can illuminate the customer's path through the sales funnel. These tools help identify the most impactful touchpoints—like if a specific web page, a whitepaper, or an email is what moves a lead closer to conversion. As a result, your startup can concentrate efforts and budget on these crucial elements, leading to more conversions for less spending.

When it comes to B2C, analytics tools cast a wider net, capturing a variety of data points, from web traffic to post-purchase behavior. This information enables highly personalized marketing strategies. For example, instead of sending generic emails to your entire customer base, you could tailor messages based on a customer's previous purchases or interactions with your brand. This personalization often results in a significant bump in engagement and conversion rates.

While it's tempting to get lost in the minutiae of metrics, analytics provide value far beyond tactical adjustments. These tools can indicate when it's time for a significant shift in strategy. Are users not interacting with a service as anticipated? Perhaps your business model needs a rethink. Notice a surge in engagement from a particular demographic? Maybe it's time to reposition your target audience. The speed at which these tools deliver insights allows for rapid decision-making. This is invaluable for startups that need to be nimble. If a campaign is faltering, real-time analytics offer the chance for immediate intervention—be it through revised ad copy, updated targeting, or budget shifts. Making pivots fast and in real time allows you to stay agile and alive, meaning you get to be in business another day with a chance to make an even bigger impact.

Of course, there are challenges. One is *analysis paralysis*, where the overwhelming amount of data leads to indecision. And then there's the issue of metric relevance. Focus on the wrong KPIs, and you could be steering your strategy based on misleading indicators. For startups or small businesses that might not have in-house expertise, the good news is that you can still benefit from these insights by working with marketing consultants or agencies, ensuring that the data insights are not just collected but are also interpreted and acted upon effectively.

For startups and small businesses, data analytics tools offer a practical way to transform marketing from a gut-feel art to a precise science. By utilizing these tools effectively, both B2B and B2C companies can develop more tailored and efficient—and therefore more effective—marketing strategies that not only meet but anticipate the evolving needs of their target audiences.

Improved Customer Understanding

At the core of any successful marketing strategy is a profound understanding of the customer. CRM tools act like a repository of individual customer profiles, chronicling past interactions, purchase histories, and even complaint records. Having all this data at your fingertips gives you a 360-degree view of each customer, which is invaluable for any startup aiming to build lasting relationships.

In a B2B setting, a robust CRM system can take your account-based marketing (ABM) to the next level. ABM focuses your marketing efforts on specific high-value accounts instead of trying to reach everyone. For instance, with a CRM system, you can tag specific accounts to receive customized newsletters, updates on new features tailored to their industry, geo-targeted content if location matters, and even personalized holiday greetings. You can also track engagement, automate follow-ups, segment by behavior or purchase history, and set reminders for key touchpoints like contract renewals or birthdays. This level of attention to detail doesn't just improve customer satisfaction—it can result in a higher emotional connection, leading to better CLVs and more referrals.

In the realm of B2C, a CRM can be used to segment customers based on a range of variables like geographic location, age, buying behavior, or even how they came across your brand. Once you've segmented your audience, you can send hyper-personalized communications. Imagine being able to send a personalized email containing product recommendations that align with a customer's past purchasing behaviors. This increases the likelihood of repeat purchases, thereby boosting customer retention and lifetime value.

Because CRM tools store data about customer interactions across multiple touchpoints—from social media engagement to email click-through rates—you can tailor your messaging to be highly relevant and timely. For instance, if a customer abandoned their cart, automated messages can be triggered to encourage completion of the purchase. Knowing your customer inside out allows you to anticipate needs and preferences before the customer even recognizes them. This proactive approach to customer service can set your startup apart from competitors. Moreover, a deep understanding of your customer segments can inform not only marketing, but also your future product development, providing you a competitive edge that is vital in today's saturated markets.

As with any tool that collects data, the challenge is to distill the vast amount of information into actionable insights. Data is only useful when you can interpret it in a way that aligns with your specific business goals. CRM tools are not a luxury but a necessity. Improved customer understanding can manifest in many forms—all of which contribute to long-term business success. So, investing in a solid CRM tool can offer you more than just data. It can provide you with the roadmap to customer delight.

Scalability

One of the most significant advantages of utilizing marketing tools is their ability to perform bulk operations efficiently. Whether it's sending mass emails with personalized content or posting to multiple social media accounts, these tools automate tasks that would be prohibitively time-consuming to manage manually. This allows your team to focus on high-value activities, like strategic planning and relationship building, rather than getting bogged down with repetitive tasks.

In a B2B context, tools like automated email marketing systems and advanced CRM software can allow you to manage multiple client accounts simultaneously, yet with a level of personalization that would be arduous to do manually. Features like lead scoring and automated follow-ups can help your sales team focus on the most promising opportunities, making the process far more efficient and increasing the potential for successful conversions as you scale.

In the B2C sphere, social media management tools allow you to manage multiple platforms from a single dashboard. The ability to schedule posts in advance, monitor social conversations, and analyze performance metrics can make expanding to new social media platforms a more manageable and streamlined process. These capabilities are crucial when scaling your business, as they allow you to maintain a consistent and high-quality brand presence across multiple channels with less effort.

Another advantage of most modern marketing tools is their flexible, often cloud-based, architecture. This means you can easily scale your tools up or down based on current needs without a heavy investment in software adjustments or hardware upgrades. This kind of elasticity is particularly beneficial for startups that might experience rapid growth or seasonal fluctuations. When shopping for tools, it is always good to understand how they can grow with your business so there isn't an onboarding of a new tool every year or even less in a couple of months.

Scalability is not just about managing larger volumes of work. It's also about having a more extensive and integrated view of your business. Many tools nowadays offer robust integrations, allowing data to flow seamlessly between your marketing, sales, and customer service platforms. This integration offers a more comprehensive understanding of your operations and customer experiences, thus leading to more informed decision-making as you scale.

Many startups operate under budget constraints, and as they scale their business, they have more revenue to spend on marketing and martech tools. The software as a service (SaaS) model, followed by most marketing tools, allows for a pay-as-you-go approach. You can start with essential features and then add on more complex capabilities as your business grows and your budget allows. The right set of marketing tools can act as a lever that amplifies your reach, optimizes your resources, and accelerates growth while fitting with your business's current needs. Far from being just a nice-to-have, these tools are a necessity for any business that aims to scale efficiently and effectively.

Equally important is how well your marketing tools integrate with existing business systems, such as your accounting software, inventory management, or enterprise resource planning (ERP) platforms. This cross-functional integration creates a synchronized ecosystem where marketing actions directly inform other business operations and vice versa. For instance, when inventory levels of a particular product run low, your marketing tools could automatically adjust campaign spending to slow promotion of that item. Similarly, when customer service flags frequent issues with a product, marketing messaging can be adjusted in real-time. This holistic integration prevents siloed information and creates efficiencies that impact your entire business operation, not just your marketing department.

Personalization and Customer Engagement

Modern marketing tools come equipped with capabilities to track customer behavior across various touchpoints. For example, e-commerce platforms can track a customer's browsing habits, while email marketing tools can assess engagement by measuring open and click-through rates. This rich data helps you understand your customer's journey, from initial interest to the point of purchase and beyond. Once data is captured, advanced segmentation tools can categorize customers based on various attributes like behavior, location, and past purchase history.

Segmentation allows you to send highly targeted messages. In a B2B context, you might segment leads based on their industry or position in the sales funnel, allowing for more relevant and engaging content. In B2C, customer segments could be based on age, location, or even browsing behavior. Using data and segmentation, automation tools can send personalized messages at scale. Imagine sending thousands of personalized emails, each addressing the recipient by their first name and recommending products based on their browsing history. This not only saves time but also significantly enhances the customer experience, driving up engagement levels.

Some advanced tools offer real-time personalization features. For instance, if a user is browsing a particular product category on your website, real-time tools can immediately adjust the content, offers, or ads displayed to that user, based on their behavior. This instant personalization is engaging for the customer and often leads to increased conversion rates.

Today's customers engage with brands across multiple channels, be it through email, social media, or in-app messages. Integrated marketing platforms enable you to maintain consistent and personalized communication across all these channels. For example, a customer who abandoned a shopping cart on your app might receive a personalized reminder via email and see a targeted ad on social media. Personalization isn't just about converting leads. It's also about nurturing existing customers. Tailored recommendations and targeted promotions can drive repeat business, turning one-time buyers into loyal customers. This approach increases customer lifetime value, a critical metric for long-term business success.

While the benefits are manifold, personalization can backfire if not done correctly. Irrelevant or excessive messaging can irritate customers and erode trust. In today's environment, where people are increasingly cautious about sharing their information, it's essential to strike the right balance between utilizing data effectively and respecting privacy. Always stay ethical: use data as your company promises, honor privacy norms, and avoid practices that prioritize short-term gains over long-term trust. Testing and continuous optimization based on real engagement—rather than intrusive tactics—are key to refining personalization strategies in a way that builds lasting relationships.

In a marketplace crowded with startups and established brands alike, focusing on personalization and customer engagement can set you apart. The ideas I've mentioned are just foundational—many more creative solutions can be developed based on your specific needs. Marketing tools empower you to execute complex personalization strategies with ease, driving customer engagement and boosting conversion rates. This can be the competitive edge that elevates your brand and fuels growth.

Collaboration and Project Management

One of the biggest challenges in marketing, especially for growing businesses, is managing multiple campaigns, platforms, and team members. Collaboration and project management tools offer a centralized hub where everyone can see the big picture, from high-level objectives down to individual tasks. This centralization eradicates the need for endless email chains and meetings, ensuring that everyone is aligned and moving toward the same goals. These tools allow team leaders and project managers to assign tasks to team members, set deadlines, and track progress. This becomes particularly useful for startups or small businesses that may not have a formalized marketing structure. A clear view of who is responsible for what can significantly reduce bottlenecks and improve overall productivity.

Resource allocation becomes far more manageable with good project management software. You can clearly see who is overworked and who has bandwidth, making it easier to distribute tasks fairly and efficiently, ensuring a steady workflow. For small teams where each member might wear multiple hats, this is invaluable for avoiding burnout, since burnout can lead to a high turnover rate.

Marketing involves various types of content and assets—from blog posts and social media updates to videos and podcasts. Project management tools often have built-in features or integrations that allow team members to upload, share, and comment on these assets. This centralized storage eliminates the time-consuming process of searching for assets across different platforms and ensures that everyone has access to the most up-to-date versions. In fast-paced marketing environments, being able to communicate in real-time is a boon. Many collaboration tools offer chat features, video conferencing, and real-time editing capabilities. These instant communication features can dramatically speed up project timelines and, if needed, allow for quick pivots in strategy.

One benefit entrepreneurs tend to overlook is the increased accountability these tools foster. When tasks and deadlines are visible to everyone, team members are naturally more accountable for completing their work on time. This level of transparency is essential for building trust within the team and ensuring that projects are executed effectively. As your business grows, so will your marketing needs and team size. Collaboration and project management tools are generally built to scale, allowing you to add more features or users as your business expands. This scalability ensures that you won't have to migrate to a new system as things get more complex. Keep in mind that solopreneurs can use the same collaboration tools too. They can help you stay on track even while you work with third-party vendors, holding them and yourself accountable.

Collaboration and project management tools aren't just an optional add-on. They're integral to the marketing landscape. By ensuring efficient communication, seamless task management, and high levels of transparency, these tools can help even the smallest marketing teams produce high-quality, timely work. So, whether you're a startup just dipping its toes into marketing or a small business looking to optimize your existing efforts, incorporating these tools into your stack can give you a significant competitive edge.

The rise of mobile-optimized marketing tools has further transformed how teams collaborate. Today's marketing professionals aren't tethered to their desks—they can monitor campaign performance, approve content, and make strategic decisions from anywhere. Mobile marketing tool apps enable team members to stay connected and responsive, whether they're commuting, attending an industry event, or working remotely. For small business owners wearing multiple hats, this mobility is invaluable. You can check advertising performance between meetings or approve a social media post while waiting for your coffee. This flexibility keeps the marketing momentum in motion, regardless of location, fostering agility that particularly benefits lean, fast-moving organizations.

Cost-Effectiveness of Your Marketing Tool Stack

Cost is often a major concern for startups and small businesses considering adopting a marketing tool stack. While it's true that there are initial costs involved—sometimes substantial ones—the return on investment can be huge if you choose and utilize these tools wisely.

As the old saying goes, "Time is money." The time that your team saves by automating repetitive tasks can be channeled into more strategic, high-impact activities. Think of it as shifting the human resources from being *doers* to *thinkers* and *strategists*.

When your team is able to focus on planning and decision-making, the long-term yield is likely to be much higher.

Advanced analytics tools help gather insights that are crucial for decision-making. Better decisions lead to more effective marketing campaigns, reducing wasted ad spending and increasing ROI. The data-driven insights enable you to target your audience more precisely, potentially lowering customer acquisition costs. When evaluating cost-effectiveness, businesses should also consider open source versus proprietary solutions. Open-source marketing tools—from content management systems like WordPress to CRM platforms like SuiteCRM—can offer significant cost savings, especially for startups with limited budgets. These solutions typically have no licensing fees, though they may require more technical expertise to implement and maintain. Personalization and CRM tools allow for better customer targeting and engagement. A well-engaged customer is more likely to convert and, more importantly, to return. Customer retention is usually far more cost-effective than customer acquisition, making this a vital point in the cost-effectiveness of a marketing tool stack.

While proprietary tools often provide more polished interfaces and dedicated support, open-source alternatives deliver comparable functionality at a fraction of the cost. Many successful businesses have built their initial marketing infrastructure on open-source foundations, only transitioning to paid solutions when specific needs arise that justify the investment. This approach allows for more budget allocation to actual marketing activities rather than tool expenses.

Cheaper, less versatile tools might be tempting for startups operating on a shoestring budget. However, the initial savings could turn into future costs. As your business grows, a basic tool may lack the features you'll eventually need, forcing a migration to a more robust solution. Transitions like this not only involve new costs but also require time for implementation and team training. Therefore, as I discussed above, whenever possible, opt for tools that can scale with your business needs. A lower upfront cost doesn't always equate to long-term savings. Cheap tools that lack essential features can lead to inefficiencies, and "making do" with such tools can lead to missed opportunities. Moreover, should you outgrow a basic tool and need to switch, you'll incur transition costs, including data migration, downtime, and retraining. In the realm of digital marketing tools, a connected approach is vital. A stack where the tools integrate well with each other can provide not just convenience but also financial benefits. For instance, the data from your analytics tool can directly feed into your CRM, providing sales teams with valuable information without the need for manual data entry or analysis.

A marketing tool stack should not be viewed merely as a cost sink but rather as an investment. The returns in efficiency, improved decision-making, and customer engagement often far outweigh the initial outlay. But remember, like any investment, it requires careful planning and ongoing management to yield dividends.

In today's regulatory environment, security and compliance considerations must also factor into your cost calculations. Tools that handle customer data must comply with regulations like the General Data Protection Regulation (GDPR), the California Consumer Privacy Act (CCPA), or industry-specific requirements. Non-compliance can result in substantial fines that dwarf any savings from choosing less secure tools. Additionally, data breaches can cause irreparable damage to customer trust and brand reputation. When evaluating marketing tools, assess their security features, data handling practices, and compliance certifications. Consider whether they offer features like data anonymization, consent management, and the ability to honor data deletion requests. While these considerations might increase initial costs, they provide essential protection against much larger potential expenses and reputational damage down the road. So, when considering the addition of these tools to your marketing arsenal, focus on their long-term value generation, not just the sticker price.

Choose your tools wisely. A marketing tool stack is an indispensable asset for any business. If you don't know where to start or how to know what you should choose, here's a tip: Consult experts in marketing like me and thoroughly assess your own needs before making choices. A tool that's perfect for one business might not meet the unique objectives of another. Remember, the best tool for you is one that addresses your precise business needs, not just the one with the most enticing marketing.

While your marketing stack can grow in complexity as your business scales, you can think of your initial essential tools as falling into three main categories:

- **Acquisition:** Tools that are specifically geared toward customer acquisition, like your website, SEO software, advertising platforms, and lead generation tools.

- **Retention:** Tools that support you in retaining your customers, like CRM software, email marketing platforms, and customer service tools, so you can keep your engagement up and deepen relationships and ongoing sales.

- **Analysis:** Data analytics platform tools, including website analytics, user behavior tracking, and other tools that offer insights into campaign performance and customer behavior (ex., a full-stack data dashboard).

Understanding these three main categories can help you get started without getting overwhelmed by your options. As you grow, your stack can evolve, but keeping these fundamental cycles in mind can provide clarity and direction.

There you have it! Starting with a focused approach—categorized into acquisition, retention, and analysis—can make the complex task of selecting a marketing tool stack much more manageable. The key is to pick tools that not only meet your immediate needs but also have the capacity to grow with you. Remember: The Lamborghini of tools may not be as right a fit as the Mustang in terms of what you require as a business. This doesn't mean they are any better or worse than the other. What you're looking for is the tool that you'll consider an investment in your business's long-term success.

To further simplify your decision-making process, I've developed a helpful chart of options, based on the categories above, to guide you and help you make more informed decisions.

ACQUISITION	WHY IT MATTERS
Website & CMS	Build and manage your online presence
CRM with Lead Capture	Capture and organize leads in one system
SEO Tools	Improve visibility through search engines
Social Media Platforms	Engage and grow your audience
Online Advertising	Drive targeted traffic to your website or offers
AI Content Creation Tools	Quickly produce engaging content for campaigns

RETENTION	WHY IT MATTERS
CRM & Email Marketing	Nurture relationships and send targeted messages
Customer Support Chat	Improve customer satisfaction and retention
Loyalty & Referral Programs	Reward repeat customers and boost word of mouth
Marketing Automation Workflows	Automate key customer journeys and follow-ups
AI Personalization & Recommendations	Customize user experiences at scale

ANALYSIS	WHY IT MATTERS
Website Analytics	Track traffic and user behavior across your site
A/B Testing Tools	Experiment and optimize with data-driven insights
Dashboard & Reporting Tools	Visualize performance metrics in one place
Customer Feedback Tools	Understand what your customers are thinking
Competitor Monitoring	Stay informed on competitors and market trends

Figure 4.2: Decision-Making Chart

A Nonnegotiable Foundation

While the chart above provides a comprehensive overview of marketing technology options, the following items from the list below represent the nonnegotiable foundation that most businesses should implement before considering more advanced solutions. Note that depending on your specific business model, industry, and customer base, you may not need every item in either the chart or summarized in this list below. Prioritize those most relevant to your unique situation:

- **Website with Analytics Capability:** The foundation of your digital presence and data collection

- **Email Service Provider (ESP) with AI Personalization:** For direct customer communication with automated relevance

- **Customer Relationship Management (CRM):** Critical for tracking interactions and managing relationships

- **Basic SEO Tools:** Fundamental for ensuring discoverability in search

- **Payment Processing System:** Critical if selling products or services directly

The key thing to remember is that marketing is like flying a plane: It's always in need of a tune-up and optimization to ensure it is in tip-top shape prior to taking off and flying!

Also, ensure that no matter who sets up your tool stack, you own all the passwords. Sounds simple, right? Yet most of the clients I've worked with have no idea how to access their platforms—and that's a scary risk. Once you've secured ownership and set up the right tools, the next step is to get organized and execute your go-to-market strategy. Even the most powerful marketing tools deliver limited value without proper implementation and adoption.

Invest time in thoroughly training your team on new tools and establishing clear processes for their use. The most common reason marketing tools fail to deliver ROI is not technical limitations but human factors—team members reverting to familiar but less effective methods or using advanced tools in only the most basic ways. Create standard operating procedures, offer regular refresher training, and celebrate wins that come from effective tool usage. Consider appointing "power users" within your team who can help others maximize the value of each platform. Remember that successful tool implementation is as much about change management as it is about the technology itself. With proper training and adoption strategies, you'll extract maximum value from every dollar spent on your marketing stack.

Go-to-Market Strategy: Ten Key Points for Market Success

Moving on from the technical pillars of getting you ready to start marketing, let's dive into the marketing plan and strategy to support your business's growth targets.

I like to keep things simple and clear, as you may have noticed. An old friend, who worked as a pharmaceutical sales representative back when I was living in NYC, once said to me, "Always: be brief, be bright, and be gone." This is how she hones her sales skills, whether it's before, during, or after her office visits. A message that has held true in everything I do, whether it is an email campaign, social post, a headline to a website, or the way to explain something, I keep it straight to the point. No fluff, no BS, just the meat!

I've crafted a template showing my 10 Key Points approach, which is easy enough to build into a strategy, and what I would do before moving clients into the next phase. If you are a company that is optimizing, then Phase One would have been an audit, and the findings from this very audit will feed into the strategy you will lay out for the next steps. If you are a company that is either getting started or has dipped its toes in marketing but doesn't have enough data to be statistically significant, then you will be starting from a test-and-learn approach.

My approach with the Ten Key Points is an all-you-need concept. I picked ten points, since having a low number of key points forces you to concentrate on the absolute essentials.

Key Point One: Title

Your marketing plan's intro page will consist of your company logo, name, date, title, and who this was prepared by. In addition, include a short one-liner that acts as your quick pitch—your chance to make a compelling first impression.

Key Point Two: Problem

Circling back to the brand strategy framework—your why, who, what, and way—you will leverage that language to lay out and define the specific problem in the market you're addressing. This is the gap analysis of the market research you did prior to launching your company, where you uncovered the need for your product or service. It's always good to reiterate the problem to your audience, presenting the setup that will be supported by the marketing plan and strategy we are building.

In the case of optimization, this is presenting the problem and the data analysis from the audit, uncovering what is working and what isn't. It is crucial to present the numbers across all marketing channels in relation to your set goals to measure success defined by what was initially set up. Here is where you will uncover if your efforts have been successful thus far, if you need to kick them out and test other channels, or if you should optimize the ones that are working in your favor.

Remember, the definition of success can be different for all based on who your audience is and if you are a B2B or a B2C company. The platforms you run your campaigns on should be reflective of that. Even if you know how to set it up better, it is still important to lay out the next steps ahead.

Key Point Three: Solution

In this section, it is important to lay out the various products and or services that are the solution to the problem. This not only highlights the UVP but also presents the various products and services that need to have a marketing strategy around it. You may just start with what I like to call the gateway product or service—the one you think will be the best introduction to build trust and affinity into your brand and who you are as a company. This could be a variety of things, like a free offering, the lowest cost into your service, or a product that becomes a trial of your offering to then hook a customer in to wanting more.

Also, depending on whether you are a B2C or B2B company, the buying process varies tremendously, so your initial offering will differ. B2C is a much shorter buying process, and B2B can range anywhere from a month to more. This is truly where you will begin to understand customer-market fit and how your product or services will resonate with your audiences. It also informs how you cross-sell or upsell other products and services. Cross-selling and upselling are sales strategies. Cross-selling involves suggesting related or complementary products to a customer's existing purchase, while upselling encourages the purchase of a higher-ticket item, such as a more expensive product or service, or an upgrade.

Key Point Four: Target Market

You defined your target audience in Phase One, so understanding the size of the target market beyond the demographic, geographic, and behavioral characteristics of your ideal customer(s) is key to further enhancing this data. Just a reminder: Many businesses serve more than one ICP, especially if they offer multiple products or services. Even within a single ICP, you'll often find different levels of readiness—some people are ready to buy, others are still weighing their options, and some need more information before they're willing to take the next step. In addition, we need to add these three things:

- The total addressable market (TAM), which represents the entire revenue opportunity for your product if it were available to every potential customer in the market

- The serviceable available market (SAM), the segment of the TAM that is within our operational reach and can be served by our products or services

- The serviceable obtainable market (SOM), the portion of the SAM that we can realistically capture, considering our current resources and competitive landscape (if applicable)

This helps build out the actual marketing channels in relation to the audience, as the audience is truly what sets every business apart. The marketing is similar, but your choice in the channels—albeit online, offline, outside the box outreach, community built, and so on—is how it will match your audience activities and whereabouts. Where do we find them so we can best grab their interest and at the right point in time? It is, as I say, "All hail the audience." They are your one true source in knowing what is going to work and what isn't. Based on each audience, you will also have segments of behavioral traits in buying patterns and behaviors. This is the secondary layer to further understanding that we know who our audience is, and now we need to understand their buying structures.

If you are in an optimizing phase, you may very well uncover an audience that you had not previously thought of based on the data. In relation to your previously laid out structure of your ideal customer, here is where we outline who is currently buying what, and if there is any type of repeat business. If there is a need to further enhance based on the data, then considering a new approach to building out marketing for the new audience while enhancing the existing audiences is the next phase in this step.

Key Point Five: Competitive Landscape

Before diving into a marketing plan, you must understand your competitive market stack. Prior to starting your company, you most likely conducted a market and competitive analysis, as there was clearly a gap within the market, to supercharge your launch. Even if you do have immediate competitors, you have figured out a different approach. The questions to ask and answer are knowing, both direct and indirect: Who are your main competitors? Where do you stack up? What is your competitive advantage?

As discussed in Phase One relating to your website and SEO, knowing your competition directly ties into Phase Two, as there may be some optimizations on SEO and website build-out you can learn from other competitors in your field. This will, of course, need to be completed and done prior to any marketing dollars spent, as you do want to maximize your return and ensure that your foundations are in a good place. Even if you feel that you do not have any market competitors, I guarantee you that someone is doing something similar, whether it relates to one or more of your services or products. What separates you from them is that you have built the narrative in a different way.

This all goes back to Brand Strategy Frameworks of your unique value proposition—your secret sauce.

Key Point Six: Go-To-Market

Now that we have set up the introduction and the lay of the land, this section takes center stage. This is where we uncover how you will bring your product or service to the market.

This will include a distribution of channels, partnerships, direct sales, online and offline referrals, paid and organic efforts, etc. Here, you need to decide the percentage of marketing outreach and distribution of each channel. If you are or have been optimizing, here is where, as mentioned above, you will uncover what is working and what isn't, since you are going to be A/B testing everything. You will see what is working, and that is where you should push more budget toward. Then, you'll decide to either optimize what isn't by continuing to test, seeing if you can increase the likelihood of it winning, or get rid of what's not working entirely. If you are new, you should do an equal spread across the board to test and understand what can work for you. Or you can start small and ease into the market at a slow and steady pace. Doing it mindfully will ensure that even if it isn't a win, you haven't lost too much of your budget and time.

As you are building your go-to-market strategy, the focus on budget and what you are laying aside is what is going to be important. Who will run these marketing initiatives and the cost associated, and what can they spend on actual marketing? Even though these look like one stream, they are actually two separate budget streams. Keep these in mind as you lay out your business growth targets and align your marketing to them.

As an example, let's look at a product I don't use or love, but as a company, they have undeniably cornered all marketing approaches. Any company, whether B2B or B2C, no matter the industry, can learn from them.

Red Bull. When you think of them, you think of their community and all their other sub-brands, versus what they originally started as: an energy drink. Everything they build around embraces and exudes their foundation of energy and community. Remember their Mini Coopers all around college campuses? They brought back the idea of marketers going out into the field.

While Red Bull is a powerful story of how a product and company can grow and expand their reach, one of the best examples of hyper-targeted outreach in marketing is Liquid Death. Yes, I know—it's another beverage brand example, but they're absolutely killing it. They started by going all-in on the heavy metal scene, showing up at concerts and festivals with bold, rebellious branding that looked more like a beer or an energy drink than bottled water. Their genius? Tapping into a crowd that wanted to look cool without drinking alcohol. Suddenly, holding a can of water felt edgy and on-brand. From there, they expanded beyond the metal scene—still keeping their identity sharp, but broadening their appeal to anyone who wanted hydration with attitude. It wasn't just marketing—it was smart product design too: water that actually stayed cold, unlike the plastic bottles we've all abandoned.

An interesting fact about community that I have also noticed post-COVID is that it's growing ever stronger. It was always present, but now, more than ever, positioning your brand as a community is a big player in the space. Even finding your audiences in pockets of already-existing communities is a huge selling point. Marketing isn't just online or offline. It's truly about being creative in where you find, interact, and develop relationships with your target audience, who in turn build trust and affinity with your brand. This is a high-impact, low-cost approach, which, my friends, is key.

My advice to you is to start off slow, then test and learn on rapid fire, and think outside the box. You don't have to have heaps of money to reach your audience. As a matter of fact, connecting with them and how you do it is going to be your biggest win.

Key Point Seven: Sales and Marketing

This is an overview of your sales process and cycle, and essentially, where you begin to connect the dots of the customer journey. Here is where you will understand how the customer experiences you as a brand, how you gain their trust, and how you support their insight with value along their purchasing path. Again, if you are a B2C company, the purchasing path is shorter and less complex but still detailed. You may not have a sales team in place, but what is important to remember is that the sales process is still crucial, no matter how much manpower you have. Once you have obtained the client and they have purchased from you, you now want them to continue to come back and bring their community on board. The post-purchase experience is everything: from the sale to the product or service received and ongoing communication.

In a B2B buildout, the connection between the marketing and sales teams, along with the feedback loop, is crucial. Sales should always let marketing know about the quality of the lead. Remember, you could be a sole business owner or there could be a larger structure in place, but as with all things in life, the communication is super important.

This plays into both online and in-store, if that is something you do. The two teams are each other's support system in ensuring that the sales goals are reached. With some marketers and some companies that I have worked with, Sales and Marketing have been seen as rivals, but in some cases not. The latter is the better option. While they have been run as separate teams and departments, it is a crucial mistake to think of them as separate or competitors. Many may argue this point, but I do believe one does not survive without the other.

In a B2B mid-size start-up I previously mentioned, the two departments were separate. Historically, sales and marketing developed as separate functions because they focused on different parts of the process: Marketing created awareness and generated leads, while sales handled direct interactions and closed deals. This division was reinforced by company structures, incentives, and the belief that they should operate like "church and state"—distinct and independent to avoid conflicts or overlap. However, today's customer journey is no longer linear—buyers discover, research, and engage across multiple channels at their own pace. To meet these expectations, sales and marketing must work in unison, creating a seamless, consistent experience that builds trust and moves customers smoothly from interest to action. They truly are each other's bloodlines.

At the B2B startup, the head of sales and I (as head of marketing) came together to ensure that communication, data flow, and leads were up to par for both departments and that the feedback loop of the leads was constantly updated to marketing. This way, they could make optimization an ongoing process and ensure that better quality leads were always an up-and-up goal. Truthfully, it all starts with marketing, so even once a lead has either raised their hand for more information or has committed to a purchase, a marketer's job is never done. Therefore, understanding the full cycle of the lead is important. This goes back to my three-part process and the cyclical nature of marketing, hence the customer journey. Once we got the systems and the teams to work like Ford's famous well-oiled moving assembly line, we were off to the races.

Note that post-purchase is still crucial. If you lose a customer after all the efforts and costs of converting them in the first place, it is a bigger loss than obtaining new customers. The idea is not to keep grinding after new clients. You do, of course, want to grow in numbers, but you need to ensure your churn (the loss of clients) is not a big number on a month-to-month basis. All the effort put into acquiring them as a customer is lost in just a few months—that's wasted marketing dollars. That's why understanding the gaps is super important. In the B2B startup, while the marketing team and sales team were racing ahead, we realized that our customer success team, responsible for onboarding, was our weakest link. Having customers drop off after two months and happening at scale was a link we needed to fix. Optimizing the onboarding process was the final step in creating synergy between departments and ensuring that leads had a better experience post-purchase, which in turn decreased our churn month over month. In this case, all it took was communication and a few instilled processes post-purchase to support our numbers for growth.

Flip this over for any B2C company, and here it is also, ensuring that the euphoria of post-purchase is there, instilling in the customer that buying into your brand makes them part of a community even after purchasing. This is more prominent than ever. Psychologically, everyone wants to be and feel like they are a part of something, even if it is a small item. They are buying into it as it becomes an extension of who they are as a person. This is real with everything we do. You need to have a mindset focused on how you tell your story as a brand and how you spread your idea of your story and brand to make people feel part of a community.

Finally, going back to your business growth targets, if you are just starting out, here is where you will need to do a bit of back-of-the-napkin calculations to uncover the expected customer acquisition cost (CAC). CAC is the total expense incurred to acquire a new customer, and lifetime value (LTV) represents the total revenue a business can expect from a customer throughout their relationship with the company. If you are optimizing, you will need to know this number, so you can work at lowering the CAC to get the most bang for your buck.

Key Point Eight: Revenue Model

The last part of this journey, Key Points 8, 9, and 10 (funny how it somehow always lands in threes), is the potential for a cross-sell or an upsell.

In tying this back to your business growth targets, this section is a reiteration of how you will make money. What is the expected return on investment for marketing? If you are optimizing, this is taking it a step further, based on the current metrics you see so far, and if there has been a return or not, even if it is small. Ensuring that the metrics are set—establishing what equates to success—is important. Revenue in an initial test may not be the main success metric or focus. You may want to understand what the market is really grappling toward, or you could be a company in beta testing and are just looking for sign-ups prior to launch.

Establishing how this all pans out and turns into a success is important to map out. This relates to the pricing strategy of your products and services, which will directly impact and connect to your marketing budgets and your CAC. Pricing is also something that will be an ongoing test, as you may go out the gate with a certain cost and realize that it isn't resonating with the audience you are reaching. So, there will be a fluctuation if you haven't hit the nail on the head.

Similar to the customer journey, there is a revenue journey that is relatable to the customer journey. Do you have multiple revenue streams? Is your company offering more than one product or service? What is your gateway product that is your main hook to drive in customers and then cross-sell or upsell them? Do you have a variety of customers who are attracted or have the need for one or more of your services at the beginning, or do they just have a need for one? These are where your revenue stream opportunity lies, and mapping this out in connection to your ideal customer, along with how you market this separately, will set you up for success.

Depending on your applicable business model, cross-selling and upselling could look like this:

B2C Cross-selling and Upselling

- *Cross-selling* in B2C might involve recommending complementary products to customers. For example, if a customer is purchasing a laptop, a retailer might cross-sell by suggesting a laptop bag or a mouse.

- *Upselling* in B2C could be suggesting a higher-end product than the one the customer is currently considering. For instance, if a customer is looking at a basic smartphone model, the salesperson might upsell by showcasing a premium model with more features that better suit their needs, which they have uncovered through conversation.

B2B Cross-selling and Upselling

- *Cross-selling* in B2B often involves recommending additional services or products that can enhance the primary product or service the client is purchasing. For instance, a company selling enterprise software might cross-sell by suggesting additional modules or integrations that can be beneficial for the client's operations.

- *Upselling* in B2B might mean proposing a more advanced version of a software package or a service plan with additional features or better support. For example, if a business is considering a basic subscription, the sales team might upsell by promoting the benefits of the premium subscription.

Both techniques are valuable sales strategies for increasing revenue and improving customer satisfaction when used appropriately. The key is to ensure that any cross-sell or upsell genuinely benefits the customer and fits their needs, regardless of whether the setting is B2B or B2C. Let's also not forget about showcasing "added value," which, to the customer, may feel like a free benefit but is looped into the inclusion of cross-selling and upselling.

Key Point Nine: Milestones and Metrics

As we dive into the nitty-gritty of today's business strategies, remember this: Success comes from smart choices, a bit of foresight, and the ability to roll with the punches in a constantly changing market.

In today's fast-paced, tech-driven world, knowing the ins and outs of your business is more crucial than ever. It's all about connecting the dots between what's trending, what customers are craving, and how to stand out in the crowd. Whether you're in the B2B game or dealing directly with everyday folks in B2C, the end game is the same: communicate clearly, offer something awesome, and always put the customer first. You can keep yourself in check by writing down your milestones and metrics that you want to achieve, then outlining where you want your next milestones and metrics to take you. Here is an outline that can guide you to make sure you are on the right path for growth, based on your business model:

For B2B Companies

These milestones may vary by business, but at a high level, these are the key ones to focus on.

Key Milestones Achieved

1. **Pilot Programs:** Successfully executed pilot programs with select industry partners, gathering critical feedback and refining offerings.

2. **Strategic Partnerships:** Established long-term partnerships with industry leaders to bolster service offerings and access wider markets.

3. **Customer Testimonials:** Collected and documented testimonials from major industry clients that vouch for the efficacy and utility of our solutions.

Key Metrics Tracked

1. **Lead-to-Customer Conversion Rate:** The percentage of leads that become paying clients.

2. **Average Contract Value (ACV):** The average value of contracts secured over a given time period.

3. **Churn Rate:** The percentage of clients who end their subscriptions within a defined period.

4. **Customer Satisfaction Scores (CSAT):** Regular surveys measuring client satisfaction.

5. **Net Promoter Score (NPS):** A measure of how likely customers are to recommend the product to others.

Future Milestones and Growth Targets

1. **Expand Partnerships:** Enter into strategic partnerships in new verticals.

2. **Product Expansion:** Launching new solutions tailored to emerging industry needs.

3. **Global Footprint:** Breaking into international markets, starting with identified key regions from data analytics.

(Of course, not every company's growth path includes international expansion. The focus should always be on scaling in ways that best support your mission and market.)

For B2C Companies

Key Milestones Achieved

1. **Beta Launch:** Successfully launched a beta version of our product/service to a select group of consumers.

2. **Feedback Loops:** Incorporated user feedback to refine the product.

3. **Customer Testimonials:** Accumulated a strong base of positive customer reviews and testimonials on key platforms.

Key Metrics Tracked

1. **Monthly Active Users (MAU):** The number of users actively using the platform/product every month.

2. **Customer Acquisition Cost (CAC):** The average expense of acquiring a new customer.

3. **Churn Rate:** The percentage of users who stop using the product after a defined period.

4. **Customer Satisfaction Scores (CSAT):** Regular surveys measuring client satisfaction.

5. **Net Promoter Score (NPS):** A measure of how likely customers are to recommend the product to others.

Future Milestones and Growth Targets

1. **Product Line Expansion:** Introduce new products based on customer feedback and market research.

2. **Market Penetration:** Increase market share in existing regions by X percent.

3. **Geographical Expansion:** Launch products in new countries or regions.

4. **Lifetime Value:** Predict the total revenue the business can expect from a single customer account throughout the business relationship.

Key Point Ten: Budget

As a reminder from Phase One, your marketing strategy requires proper financing to thrive. Develop a dynamic resource allocation plan that powers your vision while safeguarding profitability. This isn't merely about spending caps—it's about strategic investment in growth opportunities.

Map out all necessary investments across your marketing ecosystem: digital platforms, content development, advertising placement, technology infrastructure, and performance measurement tools. Consider both your internal talent requirements and external partnerships that provide specialized expertise. Factor in operational necessities from CRM systems to industry event participation.

The most resilient marketing budgets employ the 70/30 principle: dedicating 70 percent to proven, reliable tactics while reserving 30 percent for calculated experimentation. This balanced approach delivers consistent results while creating space for innovation. Implement quarterly review checkpoints to redirect resources based on performance data, strengthening successful initiatives and revising or retiring underperforming ones.

Key Points Recap

Think of the Ten Key Points as the "scaffolding" for your skyscraper, the framework that needs to be rock solid before you start decorating the penthouse. To keep this as a checklist, here is the high-level outline:

1. **Title**: This is your quick pitch on a slide. It's your chance to make a compelling first impression.

2. **Problem**: It's where you zero in on the *why* of your business. If you can't articulate the problem, then there's no business to be had.

3. **Solution**: This is the *what* of your business—what you're bringing to the table to solve that all-important problem.

4. **Target Market**: Here's where we dig into *who* is going to buy your product or service. It's all about demographics and psychographics.

5. **Competitive Landscape**: Time to scope out the battlefield. Who are your adversaries, and how do you stack up?

6. **Go-to-Market Strategy**: This is the *how* slide—how you're going to launch this beast and take over the market.

7. **Sales and Marketing**: Think tactics and channels here. Social media, SEO, digital marketing, partnerships, referrals, communities—whatever gets the job done. Keep thinking outside the box. Nothing is out of reach.

8. **Revenue Model**: Show me the money! Or rather, in some cases, show your investors how they're going to get a return on their investment.

9. **Milestones and Metrics**: Define your trackable, measurable goals. Because if you can't measure it, you can't manage it.

10. **Budget**: Last but not least, let's talk numbers—what's it going to cost to make this dream a reality?

Remember, these are not just key points. They're your business's marketing playbook, the foundational blocks upon which you're going to build an empire. If you've got these Ten Key Points down pat, consider Phase Two complete.

Phase Two Wrap-Up: You're Heading into Market, How to Make Sense of It All

You're now ready to launch your business into the market and begin your marketing. Simultaneously, as your marketing campaigns are running, you'll find yourself in Phase Three: *Perfect*, which to me is the holy grail of marketing. Marketing analytics is the chess move—it's not just reacting to the board, it's anticipating the next play. While others are guessing, analytics lets you see patterns, predict outcomes, and position your strategy to win before the competition even realizes the opportunity. In Phase Three, you are analyzing your data to understand what's working and what's not, so you don't waste money and can focus on your company's growth.

CHAPTER 5

PHASE THREE: PERFECT

Execute and Refine What is Working and What Isn't

Continuous improvement is better than delayed perfection.
-Mark Twain

Here we are, the pièce de résistance: Phase Three. After all the foundation-building in Phase One: Prepare and the strategic planning in Phase Two: Propel, Phase Three: Perfect is where theory transforms into reality, and data becomes your competitive advantage.

At the outset, you'll navigate through the fog of limited information. You'll make decisions without fully knowing their outcomes—and that's perfectly fine. This initial execution phase is about building your data foundation, testing your assumptions, and creating the feedback loops that will power your optimization engine. From action plans and team alignment to vendor management and launch execution, every element of your strategy now faces its moment of truth in the marketplace.

Before we dive into the nitty-gritty of Phase Three, here are some practical implementation guidelines:

Practical Implementation Guidelines

As you move from strategy to execution in Phase Three, here are some important considerations to keep in mind:

What to Expect

Initial Uncertainty: The early stages of implementation will feel like navigating with an incomplete map. Your first datasets will be limited, and you'll need to make decisions with imperfect information. This is normal and part of the process.

Variable Timelines: Different metrics mature at different rates. Traffic data becomes meaningful quickly, while conversion patterns and CLV metrics take longer to stabilize. Plan your analysis schedule accordingly.

Resistance to Change: Team members accustomed to making decisions based on intuition may resist data-driven approaches. Prepare for this by highlighting early wins and involving stakeholders in the discovery process.

Data Conflicts: Different tracking systems may show conflicting results. For example, your CRM might show different conversion numbers than your ad platforms. This is common and requires standardizing your measurement approach.

What to Watch For

Data Integrity Issues: Monitor for sudden spikes or drops in metrics that might indicate tracking problems rather than actual performance changes. Common culprits include

- Broken tracking pixels.

- Filter settings that accidentally exclude important segments.

- Duplicated counting of conversions.

- Seasonal fluctuations being misinterpreted as trends.

Analysis Paralysis: With so much data available, teams can become overwhelmed and delay decisions. Set clear thresholds for when data is "good enough" to act upon.

False Correlations: Not every pattern represents a causal relationship. Be skeptical of convenient correlations and test hypotheses before making major strategy shifts.

Privacy Compliance Drift: Regulations evolve, and so do platform policies. Schedule regular compliance reviews to ensure your data collection remains within legal boundaries.

Best Practices for Success

Start With One Source of Truth: Designate a primary analytics platform that serves as your definitive data source for key metrics, reducing confusion when discrepancies arise.

Document Your Tracking Setup: Create a simple data dictionary that defines exactly how each metric is calculated and tracked. This prevents misinterpretation as team members change.

Build Progressive Complexity: Begin with basic metrics everyone understands (visits, conversions, cost per acquisition) before advancing to more sophisticated analyses like attribution modeling or predictive analytics.

Schedule Regular Data Cleanups: Data hygiene matters. Set calendar reminders to audit tracking integrity, remove outdated segments, and refresh custom reports.

Create Learning Rituals: Establish specific times for data exploration separate from decision-making meetings. This creates space for curiosity and pattern recognition without immediate pressure to act.

Remember that becoming data-driven is itself an iterative process. Your systems will mature over time, and what seems complex today will become second nature as your team develops a shared data vocabulary and rhythm.

Data Analysis and Optimization: The Strategic Chess Moves Hidden in Your Data

What follows is your roadmap to execution excellence and data-driven refinement—the final piece that completes your business marketing transformation.

1. Action Plan – Execution Strategy with Data at its Core

Before jumping into action, remember that your marketing technology setup from Phase Two is the backbone of your execution strategy. Start by ensuring all your tracking systems are properly implemented, for example:

- Is your website properly connected to Google Analytics Suite (Google Analytics, Google Search Console, Google Tag Manager)?

- Have you set up your Google My Business?

- Have you set up conversion tracking for all paid advertising channels?

- Are your SEO monitoring tools properly configured?

- For social media campaigns, have you integrated the right tracking pixels?

- Even for offline marketing (events, print materials, in-person sales), have you implemented tracking mechanisms like QR codes, unique URLs, or special offer codes?

Focus on collecting first-party data (information directly from your customers) as it's both the most valuable and privacy-compliant. Second-party data (someone else's first-party data) and third-party data (aggregated from various sources) can supplement your insights but come with increasing privacy concerns. For startups and small businesses, ensure your data collection methods comply with regulations like GDPR *and* CCPA by implementing proper consent mechanisms and data storage policies.

GDPR (General Data Protection Regulation)

GDPR applies to you if you collect data from anyone in the EU — regardless of where your company is based. If your email list, website forms, or marketing campaigns reach EU residents, you're subject to these rules.

- EU regulation that went into effect in May 2018

- Gives EU citizens control over their personal data

- Applies to U.S. businesses if they collect, store, or process data from EU residents (even if the business is not located in Europe).

- Key provisions include:

    - Right to access personal data.

    - Right to be forgotten (data deletion).

    - Data breach notification requirements.

    - Requirement for clear consent.

    - Steep penalties for non-compliance (up to 4 percent of global revenue).

CCPA (California Consumer Privacy Act)

- California state law effective January 2020

- Similar to GDPR but with some key differences

- Main provisions include:

- Right to know what personal information is collected.

- Right to delete personal information.

- Right to opt-out of the sale of personal information.

- Right to non-discrimination for exercising rights.

Both regulations aim to protect consumer privacy and give individuals more control over how their data is collected, used, and shared by businesses.

Many entrepreneurs and startups skip this critical step, but without proper tracking, you'll be operating blindly. Consider using a marketing attribution platform—a software that tracks and analyzes which marketing touchpoints (ads, emails, social posts, and so on) contribute to customer conversions. These platforms collect cross-channel data and apply attribution models to determine which marketing efforts generate the best results, helping businesses optimize their marketing spend and strategy, to consolidate data from multiple channels for a unified view of performance.

Once your tracking infrastructure is solid, break down your larger goals into specific, actionable tasks with clear timelines and responsibilities. This isn't just a to-do list—it's your execution roadmap that connects daily activities to your strategic objectives.

2. Team Alignment – Roles and Responsibilities

Whether you're a solopreneur or leading a small team, clear role definition is essential for effective execution. Everyone should understand not just what they're responsible for, but how their activities contribute to the data story you're building.

For technical startups and small businesses, this often means clarifying who:

- Monitors which metrics and KPIs.

- Responds to data anomalies.

- Makes decisions based on performance thresholds.

- Reports insights to stakeholders.

Select analytics tools that match your team's technical capabilities and business needs. For startups with limited resources, begin with free platforms like Google Analytics and gradually expand to more specialized tools as you grow. Consider the learning curve, integration capabilities with your existing martech stack, and scalability before committing to any analytics platform. A common mistake is adopting overly complex systems that produce data no one on your team can effectively interpret or act upon.

Use project management tools that integrate with your marketing platforms to keep everyone aligned on both tasks and results. Regular stand-up meetings focused specifically on metric reviews can transform data from abstract numbers into actionable insights for your team. When I was first introduced to the startup world, I noticed something that kept popping up: stand-up meetings. At first, I thought, *Okay, cool—a way to keep things moving.* But over time, I realized there's a method to the madness.

Because startups are so small, stand-up meetings allow everyone on the totem pole—from the founder to the lowest person—to be included. This is also good, as now everyone in the company is aware of everything that's happening. Because everyone is there, it gives an opportunity for great ideas to be born from someone not directly connected to the daily grind.

There's also research behind why standing up at meetings is a thing. Psychological studies show that when we stand instead of sit, we're naturally less relaxed, which means people tend to be more alert, more focused, and less likely to go off on tangents.

One study even found that standing can lead to quicker decision-making and more concise conversations.

It makes sense. Sitting down gets comfortable fast—and with that comfort comes longer meetings, side chatter, and less urgency. Standing adds just enough tension to keep the energy up and the updates short. It's a small shift, but it changes the vibe of the meeting entirely.

In fast-paced environments where every minute counts, regular stand-ups help teams stay aligned without wasting time. Simple, but effective. And if your team is meeting online, the same principle applies—keep it quick, focused, and structured so the virtual setting doesn't turn into another long meeting.

3. Vendor and Partnership Agreements

As entrepreneurs and small business owners, you'll likely work with specialized partners—whether they're marketing agencies, freelancers, or technology providers. When finalizing these agreements, build in data transparency requirements:

- Ensure partners provide regular, standardized reporting tied to your KPIs

- Establish access rights to raw data, not just summarized reports

- Define performance benchmarks that trigger contract reviews

- Include data ownership clauses that protect your business intelligence

Negotiate detailed data sharing protocols in your agreements, specifying exactly what data will be collected, how it will be shared, in what format, and how frequently. For tech startups, especially, insist on receiving data in formats that can be easily integrated with your internal analytics systems rather than trapped in proprietary dashboards. They look sleek, but often they lock your data into closed systems and limit flexibility.

Now that you speak the marketing language, you can negotiate partnerships that deliver the services as well as the insights needed to evaluate their effectiveness.

4. Sales and Marketing Activation with Feedback Loops

You should launch your campaigns with built-in feedback mechanisms. For tech startups and entrepreneurs, this means

- Setting up A/B testing from day one—even with limited traffic—is key. It's a method of comparing two versions of something, like a web page or email, to see which one performs better based on real user behavior

- Implementing heat mapping on key landing pages. This helps you visualize how users interact with your site—highlighting where they click, scroll, or pause—so you can make data-driven decisions to improve your site's layout and conversions

- Establishing lead scoring systems that track quality, not just quantity, helps you prioritize the most sales-ready leads by assigning value based on behaviors, engagement, and fit

- Creating customer journey maps that highlight conversion bottlenecks

Implement basic analysis frameworks that transform raw data into strategic insights. Start with funnel analysis to identify where potential customers drop off in their journey. For example, if your data shows a thousand website visitors but only ten purchases, breaking down each step between those points reveals your optimization opportunities. Additionally, use attribution modeling to understand which touchpoints drive conversions—whether it's first-click, which highlights what initially brought customers in, or last-click, which pinpoints what finally convinced them to act. Attribution modeling helps you connect the dots across your marketing efforts so you can invest in what's truly working. Remember, your initial campaigns aren't just about generating leads—they're about generating insights. Even campaigns that don't meet sales expectations can provide invaluable data about customer preferences and behavior.

5. Financial Monitoring Tied to Marketing Metrics

Monitor your marketing spend in direct relation to performance metrics, not in isolation. For entrepreneurs with limited resources, this means

- Tracking customer acquisition cost (CAC) by channel helps you understand how much you're spending to acquire each customer, so you can identify which marketing efforts are delivering the best return—and which ones are draining your budget.

- Calculating return on ad spend (ROAS) weekly, not just monthly, gives you a real-time view of how much revenue you're generating for every dollar spent on ads, helping you quickly spot what's working and adjust what's not.

- Monitoring the lifetime value to CAC ratio ensures sustainable growth by showing whether the long-term revenue from a customer outweighs the cost to acquire them. If you're spending more to gain customers than they're bringing in over time, growth won't last.

- Setting up automated alerts when spend thresholds are reached without corresponding returns.

Move beyond just tracking current performance by implementing basic predictive analytics. Use historical data to forecast future sales trends, an essential for cash flow planning. Calculate CLV predictions to estimate the total revenue a customer is likely to generate over their relationship with your business—this helps you understand how much you can reasonably afford to spend on acquiring new customers. For tech startups, predictive churn analysis helps identify early warning signs that a customer might leave—like a drop in usage or engagement—so you can take action to keep them before it's too late. Even simple trend analysis using basic spreadsheet forecasting tools can offer valuable, forward-looking insights without needing a full data science team.

Integrate your financial tools with your marketing dashboards to create a unified view of business performance. This connection transforms marketing from a cost center to a profit generator with clear accountability.

6. Review and Adapt Based on Data Signals

Establish a structured review process that escalates from tactical to strategic:

- Daily quick scan of KPIs.

- Weekly deep dives into campaign performance metrics.

- Monthly strategic reviews that connect data patterns to business objectives.

- Quarterly reassessments of your overall marketing approach.

Ensure you're making decisions based on statistically significant data, not random fluctuations. For small businesses, this means understanding that percentage changes appear more dramatic with small sample sizes. As a rule of thumb, wait for at least a hundred conversions before making major strategy shifts, based on the performance data. When running A/B tests, use calculators to determine whether your results are statistically significant or just chance. Remember that for startups with limited traffic, gathering sufficient data may take longer, requiring patience before drawing conclusions.

For tech startups and entrepreneurs, recognize that early-stage data may have high variance. Look for trends rather than reacting to every fluctuation, but move quickly when patterns emerge.

7. Stakeholder Communication with Data Storytelling

Transform raw data into compelling narratives for investors, partners, and team members. This means

- Creating visual dashboards that highlight progress against goals

- Presenting insights, not just information

- Connecting marketing metrics to business outcomes that stakeholders care about

- Being transparent about both successes and setbacks, with clear action plans

Transform complex data into compelling visual stories using best practices in data visualization. Choose chart types that match your narrative: bar charts for comparisons, line charts for trends over time, and pie charts only when showing the composition of a whole. Keep dashboards simple by focusing on no more than five to seven key metrics per view. Use colors strategically to highlight important insights, not just for decoration. For tech startups pitching to investors, remember that visualizations should support your business story, not just showcase technical capabilities.

For startups seeking additional funding, your ability to show data-driven decision-making can be as valuable as the results themselves.

8. Customer Feedback Loop Integration

Complement your quantitative data with structured qualitative feedback:

- Implement triggered surveys at key customer journey points

- Conduct regular user testing sessions for your digital properties

- Create customer advisory panels for deeper insights

- Analyze support tickets and inquiries for emerging patterns

Enhance the value of customer feedback by implementing strategic segmentation, breaking down your customer base into meaningful groups based on behaviors, needs, or demographics, so you can identify patterns, tailor improvements, and prioritize changes that matter most to each segment. Use Recency, Frequency, and Monetary value analysis, or RFM, to identify your most valuable customers by looking at how recently they purchased, how often they buy, and how much they spend. This helps you focus on the customers who matter most and prioritize their feedback to drive smarter decisions. Create behavioral segments based on how customers interact with your product or service, not just who they are demographically. For tech startups, user segmentation grouping based on shared traits (behavior, goals, or industry) can reveal entirely different use cases for your product than you originally intended, helping you uncover new opportunities and tailor features to meet specific needs. The most actionable insights often come from comparing feedback across different customer segments rather than analyzing aggregate data.

For small businesses and entrepreneurs, direct customer feedback is often your most valuable data source—make it systematic rather than anecdotal.

9. Continual Learning and Data Democratization

Foster a culture where insights flow freely throughout your organization:

- Create accessible dashboards that team members can explore independently.

- Establish regular *data discovery* sessions where everyone contributes observations.

- Reward insight-generation, not just task completion.

- Document learnings systematically to build institutional knowledge.

Implement a structured learning process that moves beyond anecdotal experiences to data-backed knowledge. Create a centralized repository of insights, tests, and results that becomes your organization's collective intelligence. This might be as simple as a shared document or as sophisticated as a dedicated knowledge management system.

As entrepreneurs and startup founders, your competitive advantage often comes from seeing patterns before others do—this becomes possible only when everyone in your organization is attuned to the data.

The Data Mastery Framework: Your Strategic Compass

Before we conclude our journey through the three phases, let's distill the essence of data-driven marketing into a practical framework that you can revisit whenever you need clarity. That framework consists of the following steps:

1. **Collect with Purpose.** Begin with intentional data collection that serves your business objectives. Set up your marketing technology stack to capture first-party data across all touchpoints while respecting privacy regulations. Remember that

quality data trumps quantity—focus on metrics that directly connect to your business outcomes rather than vanity metrics that might look impressive but drive no decisions.

2. **Analyze with Discipline.** Transform raw numbers into actionable insights through structured analysis frameworks. Use funnel analysis to identify conversion bottlenecks, attribution models to understand customer journeys, and segmentation to recognize your most valuable customers. Apply statistical rigor to ensure you're acting on significant patterns rather than random fluctuations, especially when working with limited datasets.

3. **Optimize with Agility.** Create systematic feedback loops that continuously refine your marketing approach. Use predictive analytics to anticipate future trends, visualization best practices to communicate insights effectively, and cross-functional data sharing to build a more informed, aligned, and agile organization. Remember that optimization isn't a one-time effort with one person and one avenue, but an ongoing cycle of testing, learning, and adapting with multiple departments across multiple channels.

Take Action Now

Marketing is a lot in the beginning, but not complicated, especially when building a marketing system that will pay dividends in the long run. But it is navigable, and it is worth it. The reality is, you don't have to wait until everything is perfect to start seeing results. To figure out what you can do right now, today, here are four actions you and your team can take:

- **Data Audit:** This week, conduct a simple audit of your current data collection capabilities. Which customer touchpoints are you tracking? Where are the gaps? Create a list of tracking implementations needed and prioritize them.

- **One Metric That Matters:** Identify the single most important metric for your business right now. Ensure everyone in your organization knows this metric, how it's calculated, current performance, and their role in improving it.

- **Learning Loop:** Schedule a recurring 30-minute weekly session dedicated solely to reviewing data insights and determining one specific action to take based on what you've learned.

- **Share Your Journey:** Consider documenting your data-driven marketing evolution. What challenges are you facing? What insights have surprised you? Sharing this journey can not only solidify your own learning but also potentially connect you with others facing similar challenges.

These aren't just busy work tasks—they're the building blocks that will make the components of Phases Two and Three actually work for you. Take action on even two or three of these, and you'll already be ahead of most companies that are still talking about getting their marketing together instead of actually doing it.

The Continuous Cycle of Business Evolution

As we complete our journey through Phase Three, it's crucial to remember that the three phases of the marketing cycle don't represent a linear path with a definitive endpoint. Rather, they form a continuous cycle, which evolves with your business. The insights gained through execution and data analysis should flow back to inform and refine your foundational elements from Phase One and your strategic approaches from Phase Two. When optimization reveals new customer needs, let that reshape your brand positioning. When market testing uncovers unexpected opportunities, allow that to influence your resource allocation. When scaling efforts encounter resistance, use those lessons to strengthen your core value proposition.

The most successful businesses aren't those that perfectly execute a static plan—they're the ones that create dynamic systems where execution feeds learning, learning drives adaptation, and adaptation enhances execution. You're not just building a business. You're cultivating an organism that senses, responds, and evolves with its environment. By mastering this cyclical approach—where Prepare becomes Propel becomes Perfect becomes Prepare again—you transform challenges into catalysts and competition into context for your next evolution. This isn't just a marketing strategy. It's business alchemy, turning raw market data into golden opportunities that your competitors can't see and your customers can't resist.

A TRANSFORMATIVE JOURNEY:

Elevating Your Marketing Game

*Excellence is not an accomplishment. It is a spirit,
a never-ending process.*
— *Lawrence M. Miller*

As you close this book and reflect on the wisdom imparted, envision yourself a year from now. Imagine a year deeply steeped in the cyclical, three-part dynamism of the 3Ps—a continuum of coordinated efforts that you will refine based on what's working and what isn't.

From the outset, I emphasized that marketing is a living, breathing entity, a fluctuating blend of art and science that demands ongoing attention. Your marketing ecosystem will transform losses into valuable lessons, steering you away from pitfalls and toward new opportunities. While this book provides you with a foundational roadmap, remember that it's your launching pad, the first steps on your "yellow brick road" to entrepreneurial triumph. The universe of marketing extends far beyond these pages—from influencer partnerships to viral marketing, from international scaling to emerging technologies. What you hold is your foundation, the baseline to all things marketing.

This isn't just a series of steps. It's a transformative process that equips you to think critically about your business. It encourages continuous learning and adaptation, ensuring your strategies remain relevant in an ever-changing market. By embracing these principles, you're cultivating a mindset that will empower you to navigate the complexities of the business world with confidence. Following the plan in this book will indeed bring results. Of that, you can be certain. But as you gain confidence and your business grows, you'll have the latitude to explore and innovate in ways you can't even foresee now. You'll develop insights uniquely tailored to your venture as you see results from your testing and learning.

The power of this book lies not just in its comprehensive plan, but in how it instills the mindset of a true innovator. It combines proven strategies with encouragement to break the mold, recognizing that each business journey requires both foundational knowledge and creative thinking. What truly differs from business to business is your target audience and where to find them. So don't just follow this roadmap. Live it, breathe it, and make it your own. Think outside the box about how you can approach marketing in ways tailored to your needs and your customers' wants. Unconventional might just work, so don't be afraid to experiment—believe me, unconventional is sometimes exactly the way to go!

Remember, the best marketing doesn't feel like marketing. When done right, it's simply a value-added aspect of the customer's life—a narrative where your product or service becomes an irreplaceable character and you and your customer connect on a deeper level.

As you embark on your journey, keep in mind that this book is more than just a guide. It's the catalyst for a dynamic, ongoing process of learning, growing, and succeeding in ways you might never have imagined. Here's to your unprecedented growth, exciting challenges, and groundbreaking successes. Your incredible journey has just begun.

GLOSSARY

I know how overwhelming it can be to feel lost in a sea of unfamiliar marketing terms. It can make you feel confused and stressed. But don't worry—I've got your back! With the following list of marketing terms, you'll have a reliable reference to help you navigate the jargon. Keep it bookmarked while reading this book, and use it whenever you need a quick explanation. It's here to make your marketing journey smoother and to give you more confidence.

One more thing: The world of marketing terminology is always evolving, and no glossary could ever capture every term. But what you'll find here are the foundational concepts — the ones that everything else builds on. Master these, and you'll have the vocabulary you need to confidently navigate any marketing conversation.

A/B testing—A method of comparing two versions of a web page, email, or other marketing asset to determine which performs better.

ABM (account-based marketing)—A strategic approach that concentrates sales and marketing resources on a clearly defined set of target accounts.

ACOS (advertising cost of sale)—The ratio of ad spend to revenue generated from ads, often expressed as a percentage.

ad spend—The total amount of money invested in advertising campaigns across all channels.

AI (artificial intelligence)—The simulation of human intelligence processes by machines, used in marketing for personalization, content creation, predictive analytics, and customer segmentation.

AIDA (attention, interest, desire, action)—A model that outlines the stages a consumer goes through in the buying process.

API (application programming interface)—A set of protocols that allows different software applications to communicate with each other.

attribution—The process of identifying which marketing touchpoints (ads, emails, content) deserve credit for driving a conversion.

B2B (business-to-business)—Commerce transactions between businesses, such as between a manufacturer and wholesaler.

B2C (business-to-consumer)—Commerce transactions between a business and a consumer.

B2G (business-to-government)—Commerce transactions between businesses and government agencies.

backlink—An incoming hyperlink from one web page to another website.

BI (business intelligence)—Technologies, applications, and practices for the collection, integration, analysis, and presentation of business information.

blog—A regularly updated website or section of a website, typically run by an individual or small group.

boosted post—An existing organic social media post that has been paid to reach a larger audience than it would organically.

bounce rate—The percentage of visitors who navigate away from a site after viewing only one page.

brand awareness—The extent to which consumers can recognize or recall a brand under different conditions.

brand equity—The value premium that a company generates from a product with a recognizable name compared to a generic equivalent.

buyer persona—A semi-fictional representation of your ideal customer based on market research and real data about your existing customers.

buzz marketing—A viral marketing technique that focuses on maximizing word of-mouth potential among consumers.

CAC (customer acquisition cost)—The cost associated with convincing a customer to buy a product or service.

CDP (customer data platform)—Software that creates a persistent, unified customer database that is accessible to other systems.

chatbot marketing— Use of AI-powered conversational interfaces to engage customers and provide service through messaging platforms.

churn rate—The percentage of customers who stop doing business with a company over a given period of time.

clickbait—Content designed to attract attention and encourage visitors to click on a link, often using sensational headlines.

CLV (customer lifetime value)—The total worth of a customer to a business over the entirety of their relationship.

CMS (content management system)—Software that helps users create, manage, and modify content on a website without specialized technical knowledge.

content marketing—A strategic marketing approach focused on creating valuable, relevant content to attract and retain a clearly defined audience.

conversion funnel—A visual representation of the customer journey from awareness to conversion.

CPA (cost per acquisition)—The total cost of acquiring a new customer, including advertising and marketing expenses.

CPC (cost per click)—The amount paid for each click on an advertisement. Common pricing model in search engine and social media advertising.

CPM (cost per thousand impressions)—The cost to show an advertisement 1,000 times. The "M" stands for "mille," which is Latin for thousand.

CR (conversion rate)—The percentage of users who take a desired action out of the total number of users.

CRM (customer relationship management)—A technology for managing all company relationships and interactions with potential and existing customers.

CTA (call to action)—A prompt that encourages the audience to take a specific action, such as "Sign Up," "Learn More," or "Buy Now."

CTR (click-through rate)—The ratio of users who click on a specific link to the number of total users who view a page, email, or advertisement.

customer journey—The complete sum of experiences that customers go through when interacting with a company and its products.

CX (customer experience)—The overall perception and feeling a customer has about a brand based on all interactions.

dark social—Social sharing that occurs outside of what can be measured by web analytics programs, such as sharing via email or messaging apps.

DMP (data management platform)—A platform that collects and manages data from various sources to help build audience profiles for targeted marketing.

drip campaign—A set of marketing emails that are sent out automatically on a schedule.

DSP (demand side platform)—Software that allows advertisers to buy digital ad inventory across multiple exchanges through a single interface.

engagement rate—A metric that measures the level of interaction (likes, comments, shares) that content receives relative to reach or followers.

evergreen content—Content that remains relevant and fresh for readers over a long period of time.

first-party data—Information collected directly from audiences or customers, becoming more valuable with privacy regulations.

GA (Google Analytics)—Google's web analytics service that tracks and reports website traffic.

GA4 (Google Analytics 4)—Google's latest analytics platform that uses event-based data and machine learning to provide insights.

GDPR (General Data Protection Regulation)—A regulation in EU law on data protection and privacy that affects how marketers can collect and use consumer data.

Google Search Console (GSC)—Shows how your site appears in Google Search (keywords, impressions, clicks, rankings, technical SEO).

GTM (Google Tag Manager)—A tag management system that allows users to update code snippets on their website.

GPT (generative pre-trained transformer)—AI models that generate human-like text, used in content creation, copywriting, and customer communication.

GTM (go-to-market)—A strategy or plan that outlines how a company will reach customers and achieve a competitive advantage

hashtag—A word or phrase preceded by the # symbol used to identify messages on a specific topic on social media.

ICP (ideal customer profile)—A detailed description of the perfect customer for a business based on market research and data on existing customers.

impressions—The number of times content is displayed, regardless of whether it was clicked or not.

influencer marketing—A form of marketing that focuses on using key leaders to drive the brand message to a larger market.

keyword—A term used in digital marketing to describe a word or group of words that an internet user types into a search engine.

KPI (key performance indicator)—A measurable value that demonstrates how effectively a company is achieving key business objectives.

landing page—A standalone web page designed specifically for a marketing campaign, where visitors "land" after clicking an ad, email, or link.

lead generation—The process of attracting and converting strangers and prospects into someone who has indicated interest in a company's product or service.

lead magnet—A free resource (like an ebook, checklist, or webinar) offered in exchange for a prospect's contact information.

LLM (large language model)—An AI system trained on vast amounts of text data to understand, generate, and respond to human language.

lookalike audience—A targeting method that finds users who share similar characteristics with an existing customer base.

LTV (lifetime value)—The predicted revenue a customer will generate throughout their relationship with a business.

MARCOM (marketing communications)—The messages and media used to communicate with a market, including advertising, direct marketing, and public relations.

marketing automation—Technology that manages marketing processes and campaigns across multiple channels automatically.

marketing strategy—A business's overall game plan for reaching prospective consumers and turning them into customers of products or services.

micro-moments—An intent-rich moment when a person turns to a device to act on a need—to know, go, do, or buy something.

ML (machine learning)—A subset of AI that enables systems to learn and improve from experience without explicit programming, used for predictive analytics in marketing.

MQL (marketing qualified lead)—A lead that has been deemed more likely to become a customer compared to other leads based on marketing activities.

NLP (natural language processing)—AI technology that helps computers understand, interpret, and respond to human language, used in chatbots and content analysis.

NPS (net promoter score)—An index ranging from -100 to 100 that measures the willingness of customers to recommend a company's products or services.

omnichannel marketing—Strategy providing seamless customer experience across all channels, increasingly powered by AI integration.

organic reach—The number of people who see a post through unpaid distribution.

pixel (tracking pixel)—A small piece of code placed on a website that tracks user behavior, enabling retargeting and conversion measurement.

PPC (pay per click)—An advertising model where advertisers pay each time a user clicks on their ad.

PQL (product qualified lead)—A lead who has experienced meaningful value using a product through a free trial or freemium model.

PR (public relations)—The practice of managing and disseminating information from an individual or organization to the public to maintain a positive image.

predictive analytics—The use of data, statistical algorithms, and machine learning techniques to identify the likelihood of future outcomes based on historical data.

programmatic advertising—The automated buying and selling of online advertising using AI and real-time bidding.

QR Code (quick response code)—A barcode that can be scanned by smartphone cameras to quickly access websites, making physical-to-digital connections.

retargeting—A form of online advertising that targets users who have previously visited a website but didn't complete a desired action.

RFM (recency, frequency, monetary)—A customer segmentation model based on purchasing behavior, increasingly enhanced with AI.

ROAS (return on advertising spend)—A metric that measures the revenue generated for every dollar spent on advertising.

ROI (return on investment)—A performance measure used to evaluate the efficiency of an investment or compare the efficiency of several investments.

RTB (real-time bidding)—The automated buying and selling of online ad impressions through real-time auctions that occur in the time it takes a web page to load.

SaaS (software as a service)—A software distribution model where applications are hosted by a service provider and made available to customers over the internet.

SAM (serviceable available market)—The portion of the total market that a business can target with its products or services based on its business model, geography, and capabilities.

SEM (search engine marketing)—Paid strategies to increase search engine visibility, complementing organic SEO efforts with paid advertising.

SOM (serviceable obtainable market)—The realistic share of the serviceable market that a business can expect to capture, typically in the near to medium term.

sentiment analysis—AI-powered monitoring of consumer opinions and attitudes toward brands expressed online.

SEO (search engine optimization)—The practice of increasing the quantity and quality of traffic to a website through organic search engine results.

SERP (search engine results page)—The page displayed by search engines in response to a user's search query.

SLA (service-level agreement)—A contract between a service provider and the customer that documents the services to be provided and the service standards the provider is obligated to meet.

social media marketing—The use of social media platforms to connect with audiences to build brands and increase sales.

SMS (short message service)—A text messaging service component of most telephone, internet, and mobile device systems, used for marketing campaigns.

sponsored post—Content on social media that a brand has paid to promote to reach a wider audience.

SQL (sales qualified lead)—A prospective customer that has been researched and vetted by marketing and sales departments and is ready for the next stage in the sales process.

SRP (social relationship platform)—A solution that enables businesses to manage and track all their social communications and measure the effectiveness of their social media activities.

SSO (single sign-on)—An authentication scheme that allows a user to log in with a single ID and password to access multiple applications.

SWOT (strengths, weaknesses, opportunities, threats)—A framework used to evaluate a company's competitive position and develop strategic planning.

TAM (total addressable market)—The total market demand for a product or service, calculated in annual revenue.

target audience—A specific group of consumers most likely to respond positively to a company's products, promotions, and messages.

UGC (user-generated content)—Any form of content created by users of a product or service rather than the brand itself.

UI (user interface)—The point of human-computer interaction and communication in a device, encompassing all visual elements, interactive features, and navigation components.

USP (unique selling proposition)—A factor that differentiates a product from its competitors, such as lowest cost, highest quality, or first-ever product.

UX (user experience)—The overall experience of a person using a product or service, especially in terms of how easy or pleasing it is to use.

voice search—A speech recognition technology that allows users to search by saying terms aloud rather than typing them into a search field.

WOM (word-of-mouth)—The passing of information from person to person by oral communication, often enhanced by social media.

owned/earned/paid media—A framework categorizing marketing channels: owned (your website, email list), earned (PR, shares, reviews), and paid (advertising).

TOFU/MOFU/BOFU (Top/Middle/Bottom of Funnel)—Stages of the buyer's journey: awareness (TOFU), consideration (MOFU), and decision (BOFU).

ACKNOWLEDGMENTS

This book would not have been possible without the incredible team at Indigo River Publishing, who believed in this project from its inception. I extend my deepest gratitude to Georgette Green, whose visionary leadership and commitment to bringing diverse voices to the publishing world made this book a reality. Your experience and insight have been invaluable.

To Deborah Froese, thank you for your editorial brilliance and for helping me illuminate the complexities of entrepreneurship through story. Your ability to see the spark in my words and nurture it into a flame has transformed this manuscript beyond what I could have imagined.

River Chau, your passion for storytelling and dedication to helping authors share their messages with the world have been a guiding light throughout this journey. Your expertise in crafting narratives that resonate has elevated this book immeasurably.

To the design team, my sincere appreciation for making this book both beautiful and engaging from the outside in. Your artistic vision has given this project a visual identity that perfectly complements its message.

A special, heartfelt thank you to Nancy Marriott of New Paradigm Literary Services, who spent countless sessions helping me clarify my vision and refine my message. Your patience, wisdom, and unwavering support went far beyond editing—you became a partner in this journey, and for that I am deeply grateful.

In addition—because it truly does take a village—I want to extend my deepest thanks to Sterling Hooker, who stepped in during the final stretch with steady guidance and creative insight. Your support helped bring the finishing touches to life and gave me the space and clarity I needed to shape the final stories with care. Your belief in the vision of this book helped me cross the finish line, and I'm so grateful for the role you played in helping it come together.

To my family and friends who stood beside me and believed in me as I dedicated countless days and hours to completing this book: your encouragement sustained me through the challenges and celebrated with me during the breakthroughs I especially want to give a nod to Joann Rasamny—my constant over the years and the foundation of a beautiful friendship that inspires me every day—and to Dyala Madani and Barry Madani, whose mindset, entrepreneurial spirit, and the way you show up as people have always inspired me. I also want to give special thanks to Juliana Moss and Carlos Rangel for helping me see myself more clearly and allowing my inner self to shine through, thanks to the countless hours of work we've done together. And to Sam Millunchick, for preparing me to step onto the world's stage.

I am profoundly thankful to my students who sparked the vision for this book and helped shape its direction with their questions, insights, and determination.

To all my podcast guests—thank you for sharing your wisdom and experiences. Your stories have enriched this book and provided invaluable perspectives on the entrepreneurial journey.

Finally, my deepest admiration and gratitude to the entrepreneurs who inspired these pages. You are the dreamers and doers who transform ideas into impact, challenges into opportunities, and visions into reality. Your courage to take the leap into the wonderful and terrifying world of entrepreneurship doesn't just build businesses—it builds communities, solves problems, and creates the innovations that shape our tomorrow. By daring to pursue your passions and purpose, you inspire others to do the same, creating ripples of positive change that extend far beyond your immediate influence. This book is a celebration of your spirit, resilience, and unwavering commitment to making today better than yesterday.

ABOUT THE AUTHOR

Marketing strategist Sacha Awwa, founder of Sacha Awwa Marketing Group (SAMG) and host of the *Uncomplicate It* podcast, is on a mission to end the epidemic of wasted marketing dollars plaguing small businesses today. Her podcast serves a dual purpose: interviewing entrepreneurs to uncover their compelling *why* behind starting their companies and their go-to-market strategies, while also featuring conversations with fellow marketers to explore the rapidly changing landscape, share emerging tips, and discuss evolving best practices.

"Day after day, I see brilliant entrepreneurs hemorrhaging money on marketing strategies that never stood a chance of working for them," Sacha explains with unmistakable conviction. "Not because they lack vision, but because they're forced to choose between industry giants with aggressive marketing or solutions that simply aren't right for their stage of growth. They go with what everyone else is using, not what their specific business needs. This money-burning cycle ends now. I'm here to arm business owners with the knowledge to see through the noise and make decisions based on their actual needs—not what the dominant players in the market want them to buy."

Growing up in an entrepreneurial household, Sacha developed both a productive mindset and a passion for helping others succeed through innovative methods. What started as a background in graphic design with a minor in sculpture art unexpectedly evolved when she discovered that her analytical talents matched her creative abilities. This rare combination—creative vision paired with data-driven precision—propelled Sacha through roles at advertising agencies and enterprise organizations before finding her true calling in the tech startup world. There, she mastered customer-centric frameworks while navigating the complexities of building something from nothing.

"Small businesses are the backbone of our economy, yet they're consistently underserved by the marketing industry," Sacha asserts. "They deserve the same strategic thinking as the giants, just adapted to their unique reality."

This realization led to the creation of SAMG, where Sacha brings *Fortune* 500 marketing strategies down to earth for tech startups and small to mid-sized businesses. Her methodology delivers sophisticated strategic thinking combined with practical execution tailored for businesses with limited resources.

www.ingramcontent.com/pod-product-compliance
Lightning Source LLC
Chambersburg PA
CBHW060632080726
47818CB00003B/105